SIAMESE SOVEREIGNTY

Thailand's Political Duality During World War II

Pacific Atrocities Education

SIAMESE SOVEREIGNTY

Thailand's Political Duality During World War II

WANTAKAN NICOLETTE ARCADO

Siamese Sovereignty:
Thailand's Political Duality
During World War II

Copyright © 2019 by Wantakan Nicolette Arcado

First published by Pacific Atrocities Education 2019

Editor:
Jenny Chan

Cover Illustration:
Sven Klobučar

All rights reserved. Printed in the United States of America. No part of this book may be reproduced in any manner whatsoever without written permission except in the case of brief quotations embodied in critical articles and reviews. For information, address Pacific Atrocities Education, 730 Commercial Street, San Francisco, CA 94108.

Paperback ISBN: 978-1-947766-12-9

E-book ISBN: 978-1-947766-11-2

Acknowledgements

I have to begin to say how honored and blessed I am to be able to have the opportunity to write about a country that I hold dear in my heart. Other than short articles and academic essays, this is the first time I've done an extensive case study on Thailand's World War II history. The country's political trajectory and experiences throughout the war is a remarkably interesting story. It is not one of the soldiers battling against unspeakable odds, the complete transformation of governmental structures, or life-altering scientific discoveries. Rather, it is a story about wartime strategy, specifically, on decisions regarding selective disengagement, strategic compromises, and political duality all for the sake of preserving the country's sovereignty amidst the threat of imperialism and global warfare.

First and foremost, thank you, Mom and Dad, for always believing in me. To my Dad, who always asked if I had gotten enough sleep to my mother, who always made sure I tried her various alternatives of Larb[1] and

---

[1] Originating in areas of Laos and Northeastern Thailand, Larb is a minced meat salad consisting of lime juice, fish sauce, fermented fish, chili, herbs and other assorted vegetables.

Chicken and Rice. Thank you both for believing in my potential when I was struggling to find that myself. I hope that I made, and continue to make you proud.

Thank you to my friends who, without their support and constant encouragement, I would have never had the courage to publish this research piece. The conversations we've held—whether through tears, friendly bickering, or serious self-reflection—have provided me with the confidence I needed continuously improve my writing and storytelling. You all mean the world to me.

Thank you to my Director and Editor, Jenny Chan, for your constant support throughout my internship. You were flexible with not only my deadlines but with my crazy work schedules and everything in between. Your organization, *Pacific Atrocities Education*, has introduced to the world so many Asian narratives that have been forgotten or overlooked and I'm extremely grateful for having the opportunity to be able to contribute to the organization's mission.

I am indebted to Professor Bruce Reynolds in providing me with valuable sources on Thai history and U.S. Thai relations and providing mentorship throughout my writing process. I would also like to extend my appreciation to the following books and research papers for its impeccable writing and years of dedicated, extensive research: *Thailand and Japan's Southern Advances 1940-1945 and Thailand's Secret War: OSS, SOE and the Free Thai Underground during World War II* by E. Bruce Reynolds, *The Thai Resistance Movement During World War II* by John B. Haseman,

Acknowledgements

Siam and Colonialism, 1855-1909: An Analysis of Diplomatic Relations by Likit Dhiravegin, and *Thai Wartime Leadership Reconsidered: Phibun and Pridi* by Kobkua Suwannathat-Pian.

I also sincerely appreciate the assistance of staff members from UC Berkeley Moffitt Library, C. V. Starr East Asian Library, and the National Archives in San Bruno for allowing me to pull crucial documents and findings that would help support this research.

Thank you for giving my work a chance. Knowing that people are willing to learn about a small yet fierce country in Southeast Asia warms my heart and I hope that this short read inspires you to continue learning about the beautiful history and culture of Thailand.

Wantakan "Nickii" Nicolette Arcado
(Author)

Foreword from the Publisher

Pacific Atrocities Education aims to expand on the knowledge of the Pacific Asia War, especially on the forgotten perspectives. Little had been known about Thailand during World War II, and when I first met Nickii, I was fascinated by the stories she had regarding Thailand's history and role during the time. It was then that we knew this book needs to be written for the public.

This book unfolds a chapter of history that has not been told traditionally in the world. Readers will get to understand how Thailand was able to maneuver the political climate at the time to come out of the war ahead, in comparison to other Asian countries who struggled with postwar issues ranging from economic instability, the change in government, and the aftermath of colonialism and imperialism. Given Thailand's popularity as a tourist destination, surprisingly little is known of its history. Readers will be on a journey to not only discover Thailand's role during World War II but will also be learning about the background of Thailand as well as its importance in the global landscape.

Nickii has uncovered a vast wealth of information on the pain endured by the country and its people during the war, through stories such as the exploitation of Asian laborers and POWs during the construction of the Thailand-Burma Railway, to the importance of the underground Thai resistance movement. These events have rarely been told in the level of detail that Nickii has delved into for the past year. I am confident that her efforts in uncovering the wartime history of Thailand will further encourage other prospective authors to continue to expand on the research she has laid out.

Lastly, the groundbreaking research that separates this book from any other book related to Thailand during World War II is its ability to convey to the readers on the strategy employed by politicians in Thailand to maintain its sovereignty before, during, and after the war.

Jenny Chan, co-founder of Pacific Atrocities Education
Author of *Three Years Eight Months:
The Forgotten Struggle of Hong Kong's WWII*

Preface

Beginning in the 1800s, Asian nations were gradually falling under European rule. Yet despite Europe's growing military, economic, and political dominance in the Eastern hemisphere, one country prevailed as the sole nation untouched by colonialism; Thailand (then known as Siam). Under difficult yet unprecedented circumstances, Thailand maintained its sovereignty. Their biggest challenge would come twenty years later, with the introduction of World War II.

Siamese Sovereignty explores a variety of anecdotes that epitomize Thailand's experiences during the second great war, from the conception of Thai-Japanese and Thai-U.S. relations, the epic rescue of a captured Flying Tiger pilot, to the hardships endured by prisoners of war during the construction of the Thai-Burma Railway. Most importantly, the book speaks to the brilliance of both domestic and international political strategies orchestrated both by the Thai government led by Field Marshal Plaek Phibunsongkhram and the Underground Movement led by Pridi Banomyong. Despite siding with opposing global alliances, Phibun with the Axis and

Pridi with the Allies, their strive to protect Thailand's independence amidst the chaos that was World War II was at the heart of their independent decision-making.

Thailand's story during the second great war is not one that is filled with heroic military battles or technological innovation, but rather, it is a unique narrative of carefully planned political maneuvering that included strategies of selective disengagement, territorial compromise, and most prominently, political duality. Appealing to the Japanese expansionist ambitions on the surface while working with U.S. and British intelligence underground, the country fought to preserve its sovereignty, cementing its legacy as the only independent Southeast Asian nation in a world run by imperialism.

Wantakan "Nickii" Nicolette Arcado
(Author)

Table of Contents

Acknowledgements _____ 1

Foreword from the Publisher _____ 5

Preface _____ 7

Chapter One: A Brief Introduction to the Land of
    Smiles _____ 13

Chapter Two: The Thai-Japanese Relationship _____ 41

Chapter Three: The Political, Economic, and Societal
    Impact of Phibun's Domestic and International
    Policies _____ 61

Chapter Four: The Free Thai Resistance Movement ____ 77

Chapter Five: Tragedy, Global Superpowers, the
    United Nations, and Other Post-War Aftermaths _ 97

Epilogue _____ 119

Bibliography _____ 125

About the Author _____ 133

ประเทศไทยรวมเลือดเนื้อชาติเชื้อไทย
เป็นประชารัฐไผทของไทยทุกส่วน
อยู่ดำรงคงไว้ได้ทั้งมวล
ด้วยไทยล้วนหมายรักสามัคคี
ไทยนี้รักสงบแต่ถึงรบไม่ขลาด
เอกราชจะไม่ให้ใครข่มขี่
สละเลือดทุกหยาดเป็นชาติพลี
เถลิงประเทศชาติไทยทวีมีชัย ชโย[1]

Thailand is the unity of Thai flesh and blood
It is a nation for all Thais
It is preserved and maintained by everyone
We live in harmony with all Thais
Thais love peace but will not falter in the face of war
Our sovereignty will never be threatened
We will sacrifice every drop of our blood
And are ready to die for freedom,
security, and prosperity.[2] Chaiyo![3]

—Thai National Anthem,
Written by Luang Saranupraphan [Nuan Pachinphayak]
(หลวงสารานุประพันธ์ [นวล ปาจิณพยัคฆ์])

---

[1] Royal Thai Government Gazette, *Melody and Lyrics of the National Anthem*, Volume 56, 1939, 2643.
[2] Translated by Wantakan Nicolette Arcado.
[3] Chaiyo is a phrase used for celebration. Although it possesses a range of meanings, from 'cheers' or 'hooray', there is not an adequate translation for the word in the context of this text. Thus, I have left the romanization of the word.

Chapter One

A Brief Introduction to the Land of Smiles

Etymology

Regarding its etymological roots, the name originated from citizens calling their land *'Mueang Thai'* (เมืองไทย) directly translated to 'Land of Thais'. Due to interactions with the outside world, the country adopted the exonym 'Siam' (สยาม), potentially derived from Sanskrit. After altering between multiple names due to the preferences of different political administrations, the name permanently reverted to 'Thailand' (ประเทศไทย) in 1948. As the word 'Thai' (ไทย) in itself carries the meaning of 'Freedom' (อิสระ, เสรีภาพ), taking the country's name in its entirety carries the connotation of 'The Land of the Free'. This name, along with the country's complex yet admirable history in fending off foreign invaders for the sake of protecting their nation's sovereignty, sets the general undertone of this book.

Geography

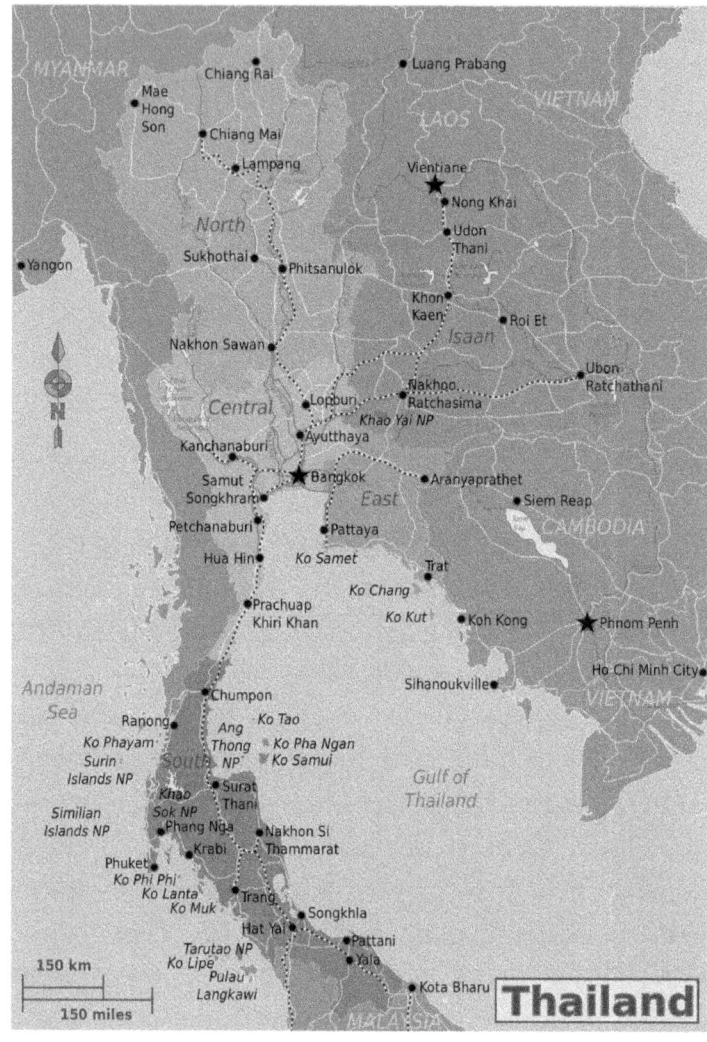

The five regions of Thailand.
Source: Wikimedia Commons

Chapter 1: A Brief Introduction to the Land of Smiles

Thailand is comfortably situated in the middle of the Southeast Asia peninsula. Bordering the country to the west is Burma (now Myanmar), Cambodia in the southwest, and Laos in the northeast. The country then meets Malaysia the southern border. The country also has various islands located in the Gulf of Thailand and the Andaman Sea, with the most famous island and arguably one of the most populist tourist attractions in Southeast Asia being the island of Phuket. The country engages with a series of land disputes with neighboring countries, including the issue of the terrorist and insurgent activities in the South as well as the refugee crisis spilling over from parts of Myanmar and Cambodia. While the country's geographical characteristics can be categorized into multiple sub-groups based on climate, culture, or typography, the Tourism Authority of Thailand divides the country into five regions: North (ภาคเหนือ), Northeast also known as the 'Isan' region (ภาคตะวันออกเฉียงเหนือ หรือ ภาคอีสาน), Central (ภาคกลาง), East (ภาคตะวันออก), and South (ภาคใต้). A summarized version of the region's attributes are the following:

North (ภาคเหนือ)

- A majority mountainous region detailed by many steep river valleys and jungles, promoting a sense of isolation and independence from the rest of the country. Various Indigenous tribes including the Hmong, Karen, Lua, and various other minority ethnic groups have established communities here.

Wet-rice farming is the most prominent form of agriculture. Climate is relatively cooler to the rest of the country. The region is known for its specialty curries.
- Provinces include Chiang Mai (เชียงใหม่), Sukhothai (สุโขทัย), Nakhon Sawan (นครสวรรค์), and others.

Northeast is known as the 'Isan' region
(ภาคตะวันออกเฉียงเหนือ หรือ ภาคอีสาน)

- The largest region in the country. Situated on the elevated and flat plains of the Khorat Plateau, it has an extremely dry and hot climate. Soil is oftentimes unfavorable for agriculture, with crops being limited to sugar cane, rice, and silk. Because of heavy yet uneven rainfall during monsoon season as well as its proximity to the Mekong River, the region experiences issues of heavy flooding. The main dialect used is 'Isan' which carry linguistic similarities to the Laotian language. Music is known as Mor Lum (หมอลำ), spicy dishes, and sticky rice are trademarks of Isan culture.
- Provinces include Udon Thani (อุดรธานี), Khon Kaen (ขอนแก่น), Surin (สุรินทร์), and others.

Central (ภาคกลาง)

- Located at the heartland of the country, with a natural, self-contained basin, and a complex irrigation system used for farming. The Chao Phraya River, Thailand's largest river, flows through the region, granting the area fertile land for agriculture—and industry which continues to be one of the country's main sources of sustainability and development since the Sukhothai period. The Chao Phraya runs through Metropolitan Bangkok, which is the main hub for trading, transporting, and business transactions.

- Provinces include Bangkok (กรุงเทพมหานคร), Ayutthaya (พระนครศรีอยุธยา), Samut Sakhon (สมุทรสาคร), and others.

East (ภาคตะวันออก)

- Short mountain ranges, river basins define the typography of the region. Due to its proximity to the ocean, tourism has become prominent, with Pattaya City in Chonburi province as one of the most popular vacation spots for foreigners. The region's eastern seaboard export-oriented industrial zone, known as the 'Eastern Economic Corridor' (ECC) also highly contributes to the country's economy. The fruit is the most commonly grown crop and seafood is the favored cuisine.
- Provinces include Chanthaburi (จันทบุรี), Chonburi (ชลบุรี), Trad (ตราด), and others.

South (ภาคใต้)
- Touching the Malaysian peninsula via the Titiwangsa Mountains and connected to the north via the narrow Kra Isthmus (คอคอดกระ), the region consists of steep costs and mountain chains. Various islands are located off the coast, including Ko Samui (เกาะสมุย) and Ko Pha Nga (พังงา) in the Gulf of Thailand and Phuket (ภูเก็ต) in the Andaman Sea. Ethnic insurgency and religious separatism have caused issues in the region and campaigns on how to address the conflict have been a point of contention in Thai politics.
- Provinces include Pattani (ปัตตานี), Narathiwat (นราธิวาส), Krabi (กระบี่), and others.

Domestic and International Government

Since the 1932 coup, Thailand's form of government is modeled under a Constitutional Monarchy. The executive branch is composed of the prime minister as the head of state, a bicameral national assembly, and a judicial branch consisting of three court systems. The monarch serves as the symbolic, chief of state, though responsibilities are limited to that of a uniting figurehead than an active political participant. Similar government structures can be found in Monaco, Morocco, the United Kingdom, Sweden, and Spain.

Chapter 1: A Brief Introduction to the Land of Smiles

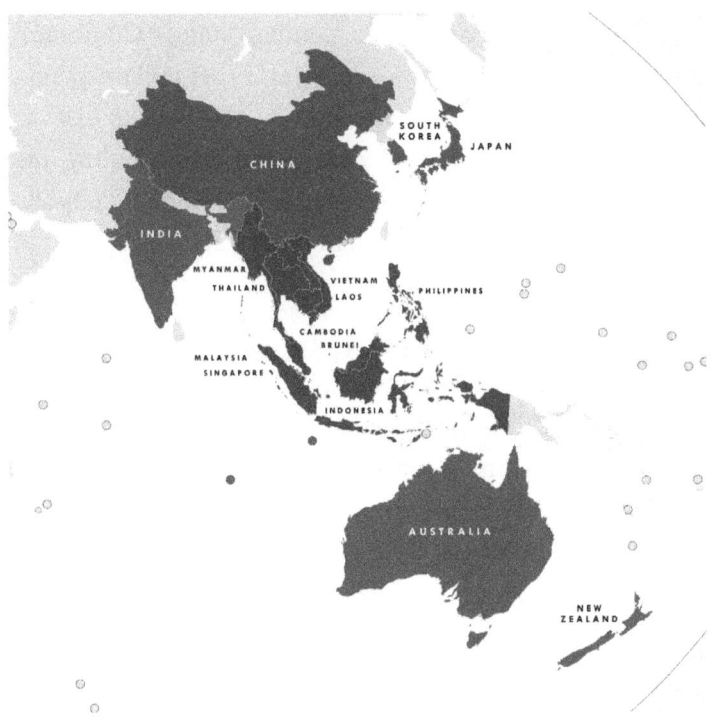

*Map of current ASEAN members. **Blue**: ASEAN, **Purple**: ASEAN Plus Three, **Teal**: ASEAN Plus Six. Source: Wikimedia Commons*

The country has been a member of the United Nations since December 16, 1946. On July 31, 1961, Thailand, alongside the Philippines and newly independent Malaya, founded the Association of Southeast Asia (ASA). Initially created to combat communism, in 1967 the organization soon broadened its scope of influence and became the broader Southeast Asian regional cooperative, the Association of Southeast Asian States (ASEAN). Today, the organization focuses on creating greater economic and political cohesion between its member states.[1] Combined, they have a total population of nearly 640 million people and a GDP of 2.57 trillion dollars.[2] Thailand is also an active member of multiple organizations including but not limited to APEC (Asian-Pacific Economic Cooperation), ADB (Asian Development Bank), and Interpol.[3]

Society and the Current Political Landscape

As of the 2017 World Population Prospects reported by the United Nations Department of Economic and Social Affairs, Population Division, the country currently holds a population of almost 69 million people.[4] The country is consisted of a majority Thai nationals (95.9%), with 62 officially recognized ethnic groups and communities.[5]

---

[1] Original ASEAN members include: Brunei, Cambodia, Indonesia, Laos, Malaysia, Myanmar, Philippines, Singapore, Vietnam, and Thailand.

[2] Eleanor Albert, "ASEAN: The Association of Southeast Asian Nations", *Council on Foreign Relations*,
https://www.cfr.org/backgrounder/asean-association-southeast-asian-nations (accessed September 23, 2019).

[3] For a list of Thailand's international organization participation, please see the CIA World Factbook here:
https://www.cia.gov/library/publications/the-world-factbook/geos/th.html

[4] Number pulled from "World Population Prospects: The 2017 Revision". *esa.un.org*. United Nations Department of Economic and Social Affairs, Population Division.

[5] Number pulled from the 2011 United Nations' International Convention on the Elimination of All Forms of Racial Discrimination. The report was submitted by States parties under article 9 of the Convention, in this case the Royal Thai Government.

Chapter 1: A Brief Introduction to the Land of Smiles

Thailand's largest migrant group is ethnic Chinese, who arrived in the country mainly in the 18th and 19th centuries and have assimilated into Thai society. Historically, the country has been a popular destination for migrants seeking refuge from the crossfire of war. During the end of World War II and moreover during the period of the Vietnam War, many Vietnamese and Laotian migrants resettled in Thailand hoping to escape conflict and political persecution. Many Cambodians escaped into the country during and after the reign of the Khmer's Rouge. More recently, stateless Rohingya groups have fled into Thailand claiming human rights abuses in Myanmar.

Similar to every modern state, the country continues to struggle with issues regarding social divisions, both ethnically and via socio-economic stratification. On the ethnic front, long-standing and violent conflict occurs between Thailand's minority Malay Muslims and the majority Thai population along the country's southern border (also known as the Deep South). Not only has the conflict claimed more than five thousand lives throughout its entire course, but the ongoing occurrence has compromised the safety of nearby provinces, put the region on a human rights watch list, and heightened international concerns on terrorism. Regarding socio-economic stratification, Thailand has had issues with the divide between the poor, rural population (who distinguish themselves by wearing red shirts during political protests) and the urban, upper and middle class (who alternatively wear yellow shirts). Such growing class divides have often been exploited by politicians, either for the sake of sparking populist protest (as in the case of the 2010 Thai political protests otherwise known as the 'Red Shirt' vs 'Yellow Shirt' Crisis) or to garner votes by attaching themselves to ideals and morals espoused by each group. In an effort to deescalate growing protests and oust the Prime Minister at the center of the conflict, martial law was declared in May 2014. Subsequently, the military junta, naming themselves as the National Council of Peace and Order, assumed control of the country. As of writing this book, the current government is run by former Commander in Chief of the Royal Thai Army, Prayuth Chan-ocha.

Long Live the King: The Monarchy and the History of Thailand's Dynasties[6]

Due to the country's intimate relationship with the monarchy, there is a need to provide a brief overview of significant choices made by its monarchy during their reign, describing the political climate in which these decisions were made, and analyzing the rationale behind those actions. Setting aside Thailand's prehistoric background which is said to begin around 20,000 years ago, the story of 'The Land of Thais' can be systematized into

---

[6] Author's Note: It is with humility and reverence that I write about the history of the Thai Royal Dynasty and the structure of Thailand's Monarchy. I do not claim to be an expert in this subject matter as the history of Thailand's Monarchy is ever full of complex decision making that, I believe, cannot simply be grasped by academics looking from the outside in. As such, I humbly ask that the reader take in my written words as a summarized version of a much larger, historical fabric

Chapter 1: A Brief Introduction to the Land of Smiles

four important periods: Sukhothai (1238–1438), Ayutthaya (1350–1767), Thon Buri (1767–1782), and Chakri (1782–present).

What is now Thailand was established by the Mon and Khmer kingdoms during the 9th century. Regular contact and trade with inhabitants of South Asia allowed Buddhism and the Sanskrit language to be adopted by the kingdom, later influencing the formation of the Thai language and the creation of a Thai national identity several hundred years later.[7] In 1238, Pho Khun Sri Intraditya (พ่อขุนศรีอินทราทิตย์) led a revolution calling for independence from the Khmer Empire and its taxation laws, eventually established his Kingdom in Sukhothai near the Chao Praya river. The revolutionaries renamed themselves as 'Thai' ('Free') people and Pho Khun Sri Intraditya went on to create the Phra Ruang Dynasty (พระราชวงศ์พระร่วง).

By the 13th century, the newly founded kingdom captured a handful of territories. The Thais had conquered the Isthmus of Kra in the south as well as vassal states in Luang Prabang (modern-day Laos), areas to the west of the Indian Ocean off the coast of Burma (modern-day Myanmar), as well as territories in the Malay Peninsula. The Third King of the Phra Ruang Dynasty, Ram Khamhaeng the Great (รามคำแหงมหาราช), carried out extraordinary accomplishments during his reign including the creation of the Thai alphabet, uniting Thais un-

---

[7] Library of Congress, Federal Research Division, Country Profile: Thailand, (Washington D.C.: Library of Congress, 2007), 1-27.

der Theravada Buddhism, and the creation of formal relations and international trade with China's Yuan Dynasty. Today, he continues to be one of Thailand's most revered historical figures. Unfortunately, the King's death significantly weakened Sukhothai and by 1438, previously loyal tributaries and vassal states in Laos and Myanmar withdrew their support causing a new kingdom, Ayutthaya, to conquer and absorb Sukhothai, launching a new period of Thai history.

Statue of Pho Khun Sri Intraditya (left) and Ram Khamhaeng the Great (right) in Sukhothai, Thailand.
Source: Wikimedia Commons

Taking inspiration from the birthplace of Rama, the hero of the Sanskrit epic *Ramayana,* the Kingdom of Ayutthaya (in the epic, Ayodhaya) was founded in 1350. The Kingdom expanded quickly, encapsulating city-states including Kamphaeng Phet, Phitsanulok, and eventually the capital of the Khmer Empire, Angkor which was forced to submit under Thai suzerainty in 1431. These successful conquests can be credited to Ayutthaya's governmental structure, which was comprised of self-governing principalities and tributary provinces ruled by governors loyal to the King. Beginning in 1511, Ayuttaya established diplomatic missions and trade treaties with the West, including the countries of Portugal, the Netherlands, France, and England. By the 16th century, Ayutthaya became the largest and wealthiest cities in the East.[8]

Ayutthaya was surrounded by enemies, with Burma in the north-east, Cambodia and the Khmer to the south-east, and the tribal states of Shan and Mon to the west and north respectively. The Kingdom engaged in a

Painting of Ayutthaya (known as Judea by the Dutch East India Company) by Johannes Vinckboons. Described as the 'Venice to the East' the Kingdom was walled off by intersecting canals, an innovative hydraulic system that gave the illusion that the Kingdom was built on an island.
Source: Wikimedia Commons

---

[8] Chris Baker and Pasuk Phongpaichit, *A History of Ayuttaya: Siam in the Early Modern World* (Cambridge: Cambridge University Press, 2017), 1-342.

series of battles with Burma known as the Burmese–Siamese wars, with the first war being fought between the years of 1547-1549. Burmese troops were led by King Tabinshwehti of the Burmese Toungoo Dynasty while Thai troops served under King Maha Chakkraphat of the Suphannaphum dynasty.

Undeniably, one of the most notable stories during this period is the sacrifice of Queen Suriyothai. Disguised in viceroy military attire (known as 'Uparaja' พระมหาอุปราช), the queen charged into battle hoping to defend her kingdom against Burmese advancement. Seeing her husband surrounded by the Burmese prince and viceroy Thado Dhamma Yaz, she placed herself between the two ultimately receiving the fatal blow intended for the Thai King.[9] The retelling and reimagining of her story in historical texts, the media, and live perfor-

(Left) Painting by Prince Narisara Nuvadtivongs showing Queen Suriyothai situating herself in the middle of the battle between the two heads of state. She was later stabbed and killed by the Burmese Viceroy. (Right) Queen Suriyothai Monument at Ayutthaya Province. The location of the monument was carefully researched and chosen as it was believed to be the site where Queen Suriyothai passed.
Source: Wikimedia Commons

---

[9] Prince Damrong Rajanubhab, *The Chronicle of Our War with the Burmese* (Chonburi: White Lotus Co Ltd., 2001), 19.

mances, symbolizes the importance of national sovereignty to Thais and the sacrifices that needed to be made to protect that sovereignty.

One of the most important monarchs during the Ayutthaya period was Somdet Phra Naresuan Maharat (สมเด็จพระนเรศวรมหาราช). Commonly known as Naresuan the Great, the King was raised in then Burmese-ruled Thailand. (The Kingdom had been attacked in 1548 by Burmese forces and recruited Portuguese mercenaries. Losing the battle, Ayutthaya went under Burmese suzerainty). While Ayutthaya King Maha Thammarachathirat (Naresuan's father) was allowed to remain on the throne—albeit only to act as head of a puppet vassal—he was forced to surrender his two sons, Ekathotsarot and Naresuan, as a token of allegiance to Burmese feudalism.[10] The Prince lived his adolescence life in constant contradiction; on one hand, undergoing military training through Burmese tutelage and on the other hand, yearning for Thai independence and reunification with his people. While en-route to quash a rebellion on behalf of Burma, Prince Naresuan became aware of a plan by King Bayinnang (son of now-deceased Burmese King Bayinnaung) to ambush the Prince at the capital city, an act signaling Burma's wish to completely control the Thai Kingdom. The Prince renounced his allegiance to Burma in 1584 and moved to recruit troops from the Shan and Mon states to reinforce Thai ranks.[11]

---

[10] Ibid., 67.
[11] Aaron Asadi, Ross Andrews, and Dave Harfield, *All About History – Book of Kings & Queens* (Imagine Publishing Ltd., 2014), 133.

When King Maha Thammarachathirat died in 1950, Prince Naresuan became the sovereign ruler of Ayutthaya. Under his reign, King Naresuan centralized political power, reformed the patronage system, organized trade agreements, and, with his strongest feat as a military strategist, led a brilliant campaign against the Burmese in 1593. Securing victory for the Thais, Naresuan acquired important port cities and territory, giving him trading access along the Indian Ocean. Through his leadership, Ayutthaya entered its Golden Age where art, literature, and learning was free to flourish peacefully until the late 18th century.[12] From being held hostage by a rival country to reclaiming his rightful seat at the throne, the Siamese King had both single-handedly conquered Southeast Asia in the 16th Century and cemented his legacy a national hero.

The short-lived Thon Buri Period was marked by the rise of a half-Chinese commander, Phraya Taksin the Great King of Thonburi (สมเด็จพระเจ้าตากสินมหาราช). As Ayutthaya had fallen to Burma again in 1767, King Taksin fled with a group of liberationist and established the capital of Thonburi a year later. Contrasting his predecessors in the Sukhothai or Ayutthaya period who sought to expand Thai territory through the conquest of weaker states, King Taksin's main goal was to protect the Kingdom from both recurring and future Burmese threat. Rather than to fight through traditional means

---

[12] Prince Damrong Rajanubhab, *The Chronicle of Our War with the Burmese*, 19.

Chapter 1: A BRIEF INTRODUCTION TO THE LAND OF SMILES

Due to his military and political legacy, various monuments of Somdet Phra Naresuan Maharat have been erected throughout Thailand including in Ayutthaya, Kanchanaburi, Suphan Buri and Phayao. In one of his most memorable gestures, King Naresuan is seen pouring water on the ground to symbolize Thai independence from Burma (top). The monument is located in Phitsanulok Province and has been memorialized in the 50 baht banknote.
Source: Wikimedia Commons

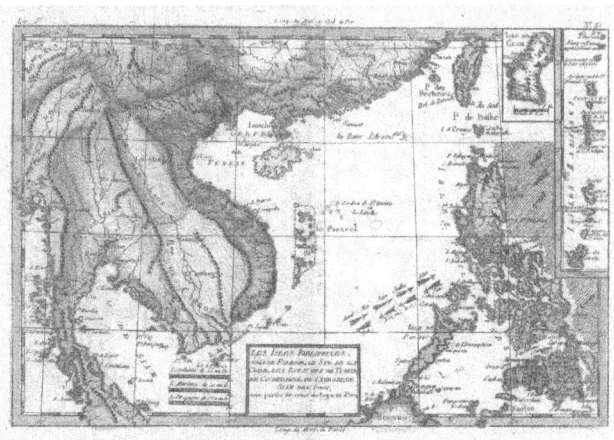

Map of Southeast Asia in the 15th century.
Source: Wikimedia Commons

via duels or modern artillery, Taksin utilized religious ideals to his advantage. Every military conquest, battle, or fortification efforts were enacted for the sake of protecting and defending Buddhism.[13] The usage of Buddhism for the sake of unification and as a symbol of Thai sovereignty would slowly weave itself into the country's cultural fabric, defining the Thai identity for generations to come.

By 1774, Taksinj had successfully annexed Lan Na (previously an Indianized state and now, present-day Northern Thailand) and in 1776, rebuilt Ayutthaya from prior destruction. King Taksin further subjected various Southeast Asian states to Thai suzerainty including Vientiane, Phuan, Luang Phrabang in the northeast, Trengganu and Phutthaimat in the south and southeast respectively, as well as the entirety of Cambodia. Most historians concluded that it was either rooted in the King's ailing health or questionable decisions made during the last years of his reign that he was dethroned and was ceremoniously executed in 1782.[14] General Chakri, also known by his royal moniker Yot Fa ('ยอดฟ้า' meaning the highest of heavens), assumed the Thai throne, birthing the Chakri Dynasty and the current ruling Thai royal dynasty.

---

[13] Sunit Chutintaranond, "The Image of the Burmese enemy in Thai Perceptions and Historical Writings," *Journal of the Siam Society* (1992), 89-98.

[14] Nidhi Eoseewong (นิธิ เอี่ยวศรีวงศ์), *Karn Muang Thai Samai Phra Chao Krung Thonburi (การเมืองไทยสมัยพระเจ้ากรุงธนบุรี)* (Tichon Publishing, 1993), 575.

Chapter 1: A Brief Introduction to the Land of Smiles

*Map of the Thai Territory during King Taksin's Reign (1767–1782).
Source: Wikimedia Commons*

As of the publication of this book, Thailand has had ten (10) Kings under the Chakri Dynasty.[15] While each of them had achieved so much, this book would only list the

---

[15] All Kings in the Chakri Dynasty are referred to as Rama followed by a number corresponding their reign in the country.

one related to the book's subject at hand. While the nation had previously interacted with Western countries in the past via trade or through missionaries, it was King Mongkut (r. 1851-1868), also known as Rama IV, that truly introduced the Thais to the Western world. Between 1855 and 1870, the King had signed treaties with Britain, the U.S., France, and several other European countries, revolutionizing the Thai economy through a newly established connection with the world monetary system.

Despite significant efforts made on the economic front, King Mongkut was faced with difficult decisions throughout his reign. Through the mid-1800s, countries surrounding Siam were gradually beginning to fall to imperial rule. Saigon had been captured by the French in 1859. Indonesia had been conquered by the Dutch East India Company in the early 1600s and the British solidified their influence of Asia through their colonization of India around a similar time frame. Utilizing their India forces, the British attacked Burma in a series of three battles that would become known as the Anglo-Burmese War. Burma then fell to British India in 1824.[16] During this time, the Malay Peninsula and the island of Singapore were also under British control, otherwise known as British Malaya.

Responding to this external threat, King Mongkut and his administration engaged with the West in a series of international treaties. The Bowring Treaty of 1855

---

[16] British rule in Burma lasted between the years 1824 to 1948. Burma first became a province of British India and then became an independently administered colony in 1886.

between Siam and Britain for example, granted extraterritoriality to the British.[17] Other treaties signed for the sake of political de-escalation with foreign powers included the Bangkok Treaty of 1909 and the 1907 Franco-Siamese Treaty. While it is important to recognize that the surrounding pressures of Western imperialism forced Thailand to sign unequal treaties in exchange for their independence, the same attention should be shifted to the King's ability to recognize these compromises and respond via a series of clever and diplomatic maneuvers.

Between 1855 and 1870, the King quickly moved to sign treaties with other countries, including the U.S., France, and several other European countries. With newly established connections with Western forces, the King was not only able to open up the Thai economy but such acts prevented any foreign country exclusive trade monopolies or land rights in Siam. Specifically, in the case of the British Foreign Office, the King sought to exploit the differing interests between the Brtish government in India and the British colonial authority in Malaya.[18] A similar strategy was used against the French colonial administration in Saigon and the French Foreign Ministry, the Quai d'Orsay.[19] These acts both weakened and split British and French policy in Thailand towards the end of the 1800s. This strategy of pitting

---

[17] *Western Imperialism and Defensive Underdevelopment of Property Rights Institutions in Siam*, page 8.
[18] Zachary Shore, *Blunder: Why Smart People Make Bad Decisions* (Bloomsbury Publishing USA, 2010), 152.
[19] Ibid., 152-153.

foreign powers against each other for the sake of protecting Thai sovereignty would continue to define Thailand's foreign policy.

This struggle to maintain Thai independence carried over to King Chulalongkorn's (Rama V, r. 1868–1910) rule. Between the years 1868-1910, King Chulalongkorn witnessed the further consolidation of power via Western imperialism. After establishing a base in the north of Vietnam called Cochinchina, French colonial forces moved northwest eventually capturing Indochina[20] by 1907. To the right of the South China Sea, the Philippines had been transferred to United States jurisdiction after an 1898 peace settlement with Spain. Similar to his father, the King decided to relinquish territory to preserve Thai independence. With the conclusion of the Franco-Thai War in 1893, the King ceded Laos to the French.[21] While the territory was under Bangkok's suzerainty and not considered part of mainland Siam, such immediate and substantial loss of land would later fuel Thailand's irredentist movement in the 1930s.[22] Understanding the inevitability of needing to cede further territory to neutralize the colonial threat, the King engaged in a new political strategy; selective disengagement.

---

[20] French Indochina encompassed five territories: Cochin China (South Vietnam), Annam (Central Vietnam), Tonkin (North Vietnam), Laos, and Cambodia.

[21] Further reading on the 1893 Franco-Siamese can be explored in Likhit Dhiravegin's book *Siam and Colonialism, 1855-1909: An Analysis of Diplomatic Relations* (Bangkok: Thai Watana Panich, 1974).

[22] Barend Jan Terwiel, *A History of Modern Thailand, 1767-1942* (St. Lucia: University of Queensland Press, 1983), 187-188.

Chapter 1: A Brief Introduction to the Land of Smiles

In separate concessions in 1904 and 1907, the King surrendered territory along the west bank of the Mekong river to the French as well as the Western Cambodian provinces of Battambang, Siem Reap, and Sisophon.[23] In 1909, the King ceded four Malayan states to the British. In return, both colonial powers surrendered their previously established extraterritorial rights and occupied forces in conflict areas were also withdrawn.[24] Two important factors allowed for the success of selective disengagement. The first reason often echoed in Thai historical texts, is that the ceded territory was peripheral, suzerainty lands that were not part of mainland Thailand. Sacrificing these lands, was therefore strategic in protecting mainland Siam. Second, as the country already had weak claims to these territories, such losses were politically and socially insignificant to Thai rule.[25] Compared to colonial powers, King Chulalongkorn was well aware of his country's hold of former suzerainty lands. His decision was one that was well informed of the price of exchange for the sake of maintaining the stability and sovereignty of his nation.

Regarding domestic politics, the King made significant changes to the country's political structure. The King transformed the legal system, eliminating the outdated trial by ordeal practice, establishing the Ministry of Finance, and codifying the Thai law through the creation of

---

[23] E. Bruce Reynolds, *Thailand and Japan's Southern Advance 1940-1945* (New York: St. Martin's Press, 1994), 16.
[24] Ibid.
[25] Ibid.

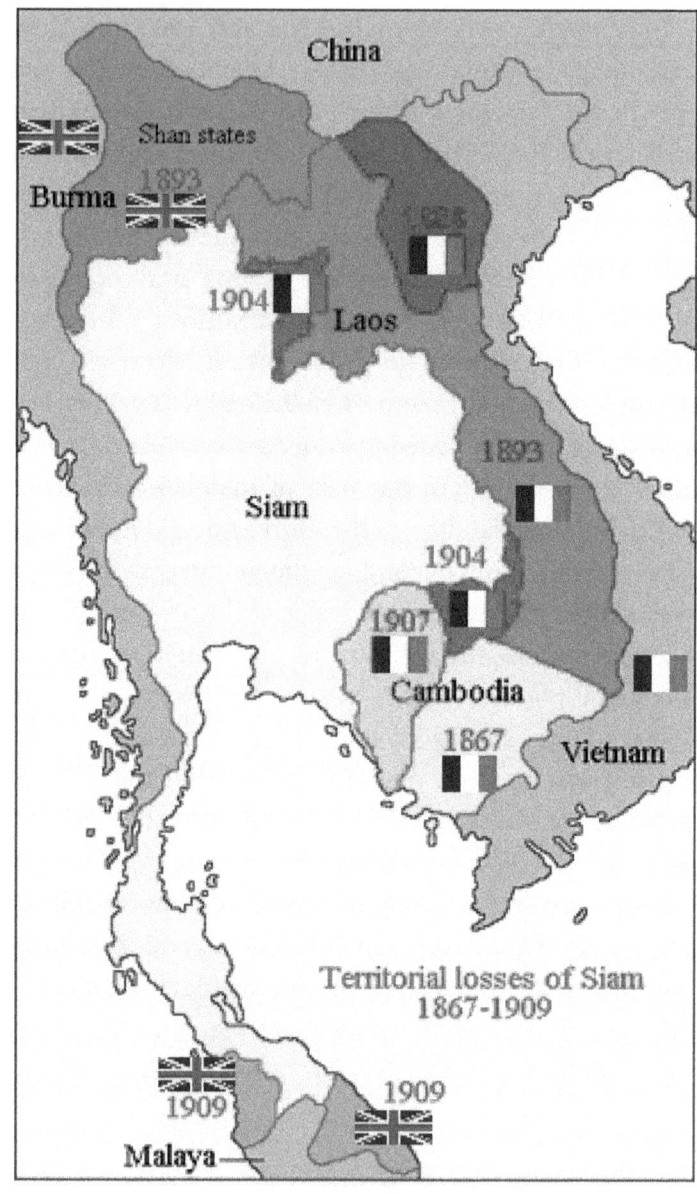

*Siamese territorial losses between the years 1867-1909.
Source: Wikimedia Commons*

the 1908 Thai Penal Code. The country's first-ever law school to practice these changes was also established.[26] Beginning in 1874, the King also gradually eliminated the system of slavery with a series of reforms. Schools that reflected the European-style curriculum were soon built, and both children of the royal family and high-level government officials began sending their children to Europe to further their education. The first rail line connecting Bangkok and Ayutthaya was opened in 1897 and was extended south until it linked with British rail lines in Malaya.

During the events of World War I (1914-1918), Thailand sided with the Allies in declaring war against the Central powers. While the war was concentrated in Europe and proved a great distance to have any direct adverse effect, Thailand still sought to provide support to the Allies. The country seized control of all German ships within the Siamese ports, subsequently arresting enemy belligerents.[27] By 1917, Thailand issued a call for volunteers to fight on the Western Front, and a year later, a unit consisting of motor transport troops, medical personnel, and aviators were assembled and sent to France.[28] The country became the sole sovereign Asian

---

[26] Joe Leeds, "UPDATE: Introduction to the Legal System and Legal Research of the Kingdom of Thailand", *Hauser Global Law School Program*. NYU Law Global, November/December, 2016, https://www.nyulawglobal.org/globalex/Thailand1.html. (accessed August 1, 2019).

[27] Keith Hart, "A Note on the Military Participation of Siam in the First World War." *Journal of Siam Society 1981-1990* Vol. 69 (1981), 133. Originally published in the *New York Times* in 1918.

[28] *Area Handbook for Thailand*, CIA, (Washington, D.C., 1968), 482.

state to send an expeditionary force.[29] The country then became a founding member of the League of Nations on January 10, 1920.

The Siamese Revolution of 1932 (การปฏิวัติสยาม พ.ศ. 2475) changed the entire government structure of the country. The bloodless coup d'etat was engineered by both the military faction, led by Field Marshal Plaek Phibun Songkram (จอมพล แปลก พิบูลสงคราม), and the civilian faction, led by Pridi Banomyong (ปรีดี พนมยงค์) and called for the end of the absolute rule under King Prajadhipok (r. 1952-1935). The factions would later solidify into Thailand's first political party, Khana Ratsadorn. With the adoption of the country's first constitution, the coup replaced the almost 800 years of Absolutism with the system of a Constitutional Monarchy.

A few years later in 1935, King Prajadhipok abdicated the throne. As the King did not have an heir, the crown later moved to his young nephew, Ananda Mahidol (พระบาทสมเด็จพระปรเมนทรมหาอานันทมหิดล). King Ananda Mahidol (Rama VIII, r. 1935–1946) would spend a majority of his reign—and throughout the events of World War II—completing his studies in Switzerland.

Through this summary of Thailand's history before World War II, it is undeniable that the underlying objective of each monarchy's rule is the protection of its Kingdom from foreign invasion. From the fight for independence from the Khmer rule to concessions made to foreign powers, even to the balancing act between both Allied and Axis

---

[29] Ibid., 133-134.

powers which will be the main focus of this book, it is highly noteworthy that the country had succeeded, significantly due to the leadership of its monarchy.

To conclude, it is important to note that the country prides itself the most, arguably more than any other trait, of its status in being one of the only countries in the world, most importantly, the only country in Southeast Asia that was never colonized. While surrounding Asian countries were under colonial rule, Thailand was able to maintain its sovereignty. Furthermore, Thailand managed to avoid the wave of communist revolutions that took control of those very same neighboring countries during the 1960s and 1970s. It is this fight for independence through strategies of selective disengagement, territorial compromise, and political duality, all for the sake of protecting the nation and its people, which is the basis of this book.

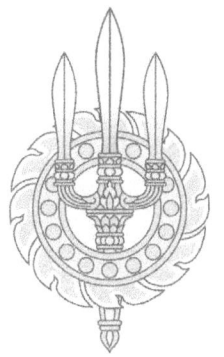 

(Left) Emblem of the House of Chakri. The three-tip trident ('Trisula') is intertwined with the disk ('Chakra') and are the weapon of choice for the deity Vishnu. (Right) The original 1932 constitution of Siam displayed at the Thai Parliament Museum in Bangkok.
Source: Wikimedia Commons

Chapter Two

The Thai-Japanese Relationship

The Budding of a New Thai-Japanese Relationship

Early Thailand and Japanese contact can be traced to the 15th century. The two country's early interactions were transactional, ultimately boiling down to trade and overseas cultural missions. One official who sparked the charge for extensive Japanese-Thai alliance was Inagaki Manjiro, the General Secretary of the Oriental Association (Tōyō Kyōkai). After the successful invasion and capture of Manchuria (Manchukuo) in 1895, Inagaki promoted the idea of creating a sphere of influence in the Pacific. In particular, Inagaki sought to create a diplomatic defense in the region and lobbied the Japanese government to establish relations with Siam.[1] He was chosen to represent Japan at the foreign conference, including an 1897-1898 negotiation regarding extraterritoriality rights. What was most impressive was Inagaki's

---

[1] Reynolds, *Thailand and Japan's Southern Advance*, 5-7.

ability to break the monopoly of European advisory positions within the Siamese government.[2] King Chulalongkorn was well aware of Japan's growing influence in the West, and in 1902, proposed a defense alliance with the country. While Thai-Japanese relations remained relatively quiet after the King's death, the 1930s and the events that defined the decade would serve to lay the foundation for the Japanese Empire's Southern Expansion Doctrine known as Nanshin-ron.

As mentioned previously, the 1932 coup d'état transformed the fabric of Thai society, replacing the system of Absolute Monarchy with a Constitutional Monarchy and introducing the country to its very first constitution. In addition, the Promoters (i.e. Thai elites, military personnel, and intellectuals who were involved in the coup) (ผู้ก่อการ) called for the adoption of a six-point revolutionary principles (หลัก 6 ประการของคณะราษฎร): (1) Absolute national independence (ประชาธิปไตย), (2) The maintenance of national security (อิสรภาพ), (3) The promotion of a national economic plan (กสิกรรม) (4) Equality for all (เสมอภาค), (5) The promotion of complete liberty and freedom to the extent as to which note impede on the four aforementioned principles (เสรีภาพ) (6) Education to all (การศึกษา).[3]

Despite tremendous accomplishments, the Promoters split due to alienating ideological differences with Phi-

---

[2] Ibid.

[3] Khana Ratsadon, Khana Ratsadon Announcement Issue 1. (คณะราษฎร, ประกาศคณะราษฎร ฉบับที่ ๑)

bun leading the military faction and Pridi leading the civilian faction. French-educated lawyer keen on socialist theory, Pridi hoped to nationalize the Thai economy. As a newly appointed Minister of Finance, he presented initiatives that focused on balancing the economy, creating a social security net, establishing universal basic income, and alleviating poverty within the country. Unfortunately, such radical ideas garnered opposition from both Phibun and royalists and they were soon deemed communist. The National Assembly was soon dissolved and Pridi was forced into exile.

While retreating to France, Pridi's polar opposite and political foil, Phibun, rose to prominence. Working his way up from cadet school to become an artillery officer, Phibun led a second successful coup in June 1933 and quashed the October 1933 Boworadet rebellion led by royalist Prince Boworade and his allies. Through these accomplishments, Phibun emerged as a Thai national hero and by 1938, assumed the position of both Prime Minister and Commander of the Royal Siamese Army. The power struggle between both Pridi and Phibun is not only an important cornerstone to the growing modernization of Thailand, but such tensions provide context into the eventual Thai-Japanese alliance as well as the formation of the Free Thai movement, a movement that largely worked to oppose and counteract that very alliance.

While no one can deny that various incidents and events eventually culminated to the Thai-Japanese partnership, there are two specific events that cemented such partnership.

The Vote

Thailand's unexpected international response to Japan's seizure of Manchuria proved to be a pivotal event in building future Thai-Japanese relations. Since the beginning of the Meiji period in 1868, Japan had successfully consolidated its power and international influence. Despite their economic and political growth, however, post-World War I treaties and policies enacted by the West proved to invalidated Japan's membership into the great powers. During the 1919 Paris Peace Conference, Japan's attempt to include a racial equality clause (人種的差別撤廃提案) to the Covenant of the League of Nations was blocked by Western officials, specifically the United States and Great Britain.[4]

A few years later, the United States terminated the 1902 Ango-Japanese alliance and effective banned Japanese immigration through the enactment of the 1924 National Origins Act, or Johnson-Reed Act, although it didn't state explicitly, it was aimed at Asian immigrants. The act imposed fines on transportation companies that landed foreigners in violation of U.S. immigrants and barred limited immigrants from Asian countries, especially Japanese immigrants. The Act, passed in the House with a 323 to 71 vote, reduced the immigration cap to 165,000 individuals per year with the country cap restricted to 2% of the foreign-born population of that

---

[4] Naoko Simazu, *Japan, Race and Equality: The Racial Equality Proposal of 1919.* (Routledge, 2002), 1.

Chapter 2: THE THAI-JAPANESE RELATIONSHIP

nationality listed on the 1890 census.[5] As the legislation intentionally used the 1890 census over the 1910 census, this caused a highly disproportionate representation of Northern and Western Europeans over Eastern Europeans and individuals from the Asia-Pacific triangle. Since the census was recorded before the Great Wave of Immigration that saw a substantial increase in Asian, specifically Japanese, immigration during the turn of the century, the immigration process was skewed to favor new immigrants from Northern and Western Europe and restrict those from Asia.

The legislation was written under the undercurrent of the 'Yellow Peril', a xenophobic ideology-turned-campaign that believed East Asian nationals were a danger to the United States. The campaign, emerging from fears of Japan's growing global influence as well as prior vindication for anti-Chinese sentiments (as reflected in the U.S.' enactment of the 1882 Chinese Exclusion Act), engaged in acts of violence against Japanese nationals. This included mob assaults, forcible expulsion from farming areas, the prohibition of adopting alternative occupational paths, and social segregation. These discriminatory acts were soon institutionalized into law. Lobbyists pressured lawmakers to include a clause that prohibited any 'aliens ineligible for citizenship' to immigrate to the U.S., prohibiting future Japanese immigration and prevented existing Japanese nationals to naturalize. Such discriminatory legislation defined the turning point of

---

[5] Walter A. Ewing, "Opportunity and Exclusion: A Brief History of U.S. Immigration Policy," *Immigration Policy Center* (2012): 1-7.

U.S.-Japanese relations, with feelings of frustration, betrayal, and humiliation transforming into a physical assault on U.S. territory with the attack on Pearl Harbor later during WW2.

Other factors contributed to Japan's growing animosity towards the West and its decision to side with the Axis during the war. The effects of the Great Depression and the Great Kanto Earthquake of 1923 plunged Japan through a series of both political and financial instabilities. The results of this instability giving rise to the strength of financial conglomerates known as zaibatsus (財閥), who would later go to fund Japan's military-industrial complex during the war. With both external pressures from Western foreign policies as well as internal pressures from continuously growing ultranationalist campaigns, Japan soon found itself pursuing the expansionist route. Feeling alienated from the world, Japan shifting its focus from isolationism to full-on invasion.

Japan soon launched an attack against China known as the Mukden Incident (beginning on September 18, 1931), proceeding with a full invasion of Manchuria six months later.[6] In February 1933, a vote was held in the League of Nations to condemn the Japanese occupation

---

[6] The Mukden Incident was a staged attack initiated by the Japanese Imperial Army where dynamite was detonated along the rail line near Mukden (now modern day Shenyang). As the line was owned by Japan's South Manchuria Railway, the Imperial Army framed the attack on the Chinese and proceeded with a full invasion of the region of Manchuria. More information can be read about the Mukden Incident and the seizure of Manchuria in Ian Nish's work *The History of Manchuria, 1840-1948, Vol. I & II: A Sino-Russo-Japanese Triangle*.

of Manchuria. In protest, the Japanese delegation walked out of the room. The only country that chose to abstain, was Thailand. While arguably the decision seemed to stem from Thailand's wish to stay neutral, the act served as a symbol of solidarity for the Japanese.[7]

Phibun capitalized on this conviction. Through political strategy, he used the growing Japanese interest in Thailand as leverage against the U.S. and Britain, who were insistent that Thailand not yielding to Japanese advances. Under the leadership of Ambassador Sir Josiah Crosby (served 1934–1941), Britain built stronger ties with Siam and competed against the Japanese for influence in Bangkok. Utilizing this newly found leverage, Thailand convinced the British to surrender extraterritoriality in Siam as well as other previously held privileges. Further playing on the opposing countries' anxieties, Phibun fabricated and exaggerated threats of 'pro-Japanese' or 'pro-British' alliances that threatened to overthrow Thailand's political order. Towards the British and French, Phibun exaggerated stories of inducements offered by the Japanese, such as their willingness to grant Thailand areas of Laos and Cambodia should the Japanese conquer Indochina.[8] Towards the Japanese, Phibun commented on tempting treaties proposed by the two Western states. In one incident, Phibun had proposed a nonaggression treaty with both France and Britain.

---

[7] Reynolds, *Thailand and Japan's Southern Advance*, 11.
[8] Richard James Aldrich, *The Key to the South: Britain, the United States, and Thailand During the Approach of the Pacific War, 1929-1942* (Oxford: Oxford University Press, 1993), 20.

Hearing of this news, Japanese officials swiftly drafted a similar treaty, and when hearing that the pact would be signed on the same day of June 12, 1940, organized a signing in Tokyo two time zones ahead of Bangkok.[9] While Phibun knew that the pacts would have no binding effects, this boosted his reputation amongst Japanese officials who now believed he was favorably disposed towards them.[10]

These calculated negotiation tactics serve as an opposition to the often misleading narrative that Phibun was purely "pro-Japanese." Critics often have confounded Phibun's recognition of the changing political climate and his adjustment to align the country according to such shifting balance of power with the black and white analysis of him

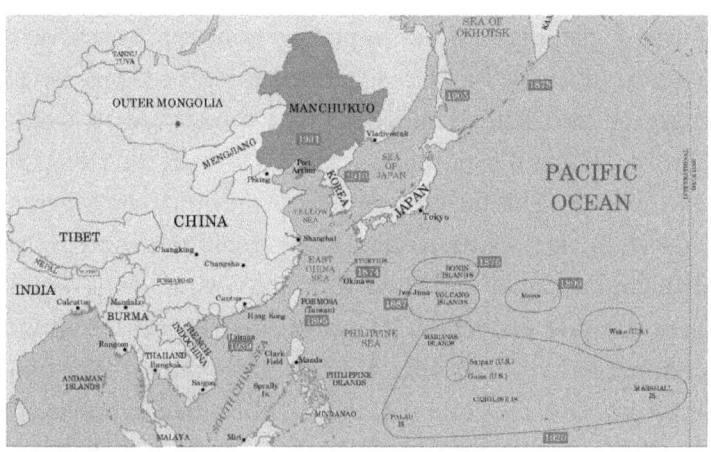

Japanese Occupation of Manchuria highlighted in red as well as the Japanese Sphere of Influence with accompanying dates.
Source: Wikimedia Commons

---

[9] Ibid., 225.
[10] Reynolds, *Thailand and Japan's Southern Advance*, 16.

becoming a Japanese puppet. This theory is further explained in the second point regarding concessions.

The Concessions

While the previous section dispelled the literature that one-sidedly marked Phibun as Thailand's major villain during the war, it is important to note his underlying agenda while he was Prime Minister. To Phibun, and the military faction as a whole, reclaiming and restoring formerly lost territories was part of a broader nationalist plan. Phibun utilized what Professor Bruce E. Reynolds defines as "militant irredentist nationalism" to rally public support for his policy agendas and justify the country's territorial claims.[11] One of the first assertions for these claims was the Defense Ministry's circulation of maps underscoring lost territories.[12] In the coming years, funding was funneled into producing militaristic films and dramas, such as the film *Luad Thaharn Thai* 'เลือดทะหาไทย' (The Blood of Thai Soldiers) in 1935 and the TV series *Luad Suphan* 'เลือดสุพรรณ' (The Blood of Suphan) in 1936.

Other components of Phibun's nationalism included popularizing traditional Thai culture including attire, songs, and traditional dance, declaring Thai as the official language, and reverting the country's name from Siam to

---

[11] E. Bruce Reynolds, "Phibun Songkhram and Thai Nationalism in the Fascist Era," *European Journal of East Asian Studies*, Volume 3. (2004): 106.
[12] Ibid.

Thailand.¹³ In other words, he sought to unite the country under a singular custom, tradition, and faith.

In the wake of French capitulations by the hands of the Germans, Phibun and irredentist jumped on the opportunity to lay claims for concessions. Phibun launched an invasion of the French vassal state territories in early October 1940, an event which would become known as the Franco-Thai War (กรณีพิพาทอินโดจีน). While the swift action to conquer the territories can be seen as Phibun's desire to promote his nationalist agenda, an even more important reason was Thailand's refusal to have the territories fall into Japanese hands. Thailand was still wary about the Japanese offensive in Indochina and proposed to Monsieur Leppisier, the French Minister in Bangkok, for a potential French-Thai alliance to fend off Japanese advancement.¹⁴ Humiliated and confused by their defeats in Europe and Asia, France was unable to respond to the call for cooperation.¹⁵ Their failure to partner with Thailand during this time would cost them significant territory both during and after the conclusion of the war.

The British recognized the strides made in Thai foreign relations. In a meeting with the Thai Deputy Foreign Minister, Direk Jayanama, Crosby spoke to the

---

¹³ David K. Wyatt, *Thailand: A Short History* (New Haven: Yale University Press, 2003), 256-257.
¹⁴ Nik Anuar Nik Mahmud, "British Policy and Thailand, 1939-1940," *Jebat: Malaysian Journal of History, Politics and Strategic Studies*, Volume 9 (1979): 189.
¹⁵ Reynolds, "Phibun Songkhram and Thai Nationalism in the Fascist Era," 37.

Chapter 2: THE THAI-JAPANESE RELATIONSHIP

preference of Thai acquisition of Indochinese territories over that of the Japanese stating:

> *"If it came to the worst with France and if Thailand were in consequence to set about recovering any of her lost territories to the east, it would never do for her to receive them as gifts at the hands of the Japanese, who would assuredly impose as a condition for making it that Thailand should recognize the so-called 'New Order' in East Asia. It would be better for the Thais to come by their territorial acquisitions as the natural heirs of the French, and not as a beneficiary of the Japanese".* [16]

As part of their plan, Thailand then shifted their energy towards the Japanese. In February 1941, Phibun claimed his administration was on the verge of being ousted by a "pro-British" faction and called for Japanese assistance in supporting Thailand's claim for concessions.[17] Japanese officials were convinced of Phibun's declaration, raising concerns of the British potential to overthrow Phibun's regime (who by now, the Japanese saw as a leader of the pro-Japanese clique) subsequently causing a political and financial panic.[18] In reality, the British were recovering from the loss of over 68,000 men during the

---

[16] Crosby to FO, July 5, 1940, F3690. Note: All Foreign Office correspondence are taken from Nik Anuar B. Nik Mahmud's article *British Policy and Thailand, 1939-1940.*

[17] Ibid., 47.

[18] Bōeichō Bōei Kenshujo Senshishitsu, *Daibon' ei rikugunbu (The Army Section of Imperial General Head-quarters)* (Tokyo, 1968-1974), 189.

French campaign, signing lend-lease agreements with the U.S. due to the depletion of their liquid currency, and experiencing the loss of their Thai foreign minister due to Sir Josiah Crosby's resignation.

Japan responded through mediating negotiations between Thailand and the French. On March 11, 1941, Japan hosted a conference in Saigon, Vietnam, brokering a deal requesting a ceasefire between Marshal Philippe Petain from France and Generals from Thailand near the vassal state territories. The ceasefire was signed on January 31, 1941, with an armistice deal arranged to be effective two days later. By May, a peace treaty between the two parties was signed in Tokyo, where France agreed to relinquish the disputed territories. France ceded Northwestern Cambodia and Laotian territory west of the Mekong river to Thailand. This included Battambang and Pailin (renamed Phra Tabong Province), Siem Reap, Banteay Meanchey and Oddar Meanchey (incorporated as Phibunsongkhram Province) and Xaignabouli and Luang Prabang Province (which was renamed to Lan Chang Province).[19]

Only several years later did the Japanese realize they were part of Thailand's pawns all along. While Thailand gained over 54,000 kilometers of territory—much to the contentment of Phibun and irredentist—Japanese officials soon began to realize that Thai perception towards

---

[19] Kobkua Suwannathat-Pian, "Thai Wartime Leadership Reconsidered: Phibun and Pridi Kobkua Suwannathat-Pian," *Journal of Southeast Asian Studies* Volume 27, Issue 1. (The Japanese Occupation in Southeast Asia), (1996), 170.

them remained ambivalent. There seemed to be a lack of gratitude despite Japan's goodwill. Japan would only realize years later that Thailand had skillfully bolstered Japan's ego and exaggerated their pro-Japanese stance during the mediation for the sake of advancing their own interests. Their loyalty remained tied to their country, not their 'Asian brother'.

Ultimate Decisions

By 1939, the Axis Powers had acquired significant territory. The Germans had captured Czechoslovakia, Italy had begun occupying Albania, and Japan had successfully seized control of both the Hainan and Spratly Islands. By September, the Germans launched full-fledged assault against Poland, causing both France and Britain to declare war. At this point, Thailand sought to reach out to Allies for assistance. Despite his awareness of Thailand's calculating strategy in the war, Sir Josiah Crosby called for Britain's Foreign Office to come to Thailand's aid, stating that the country's neutrality "depends on the last resort upon the degree of armed strength which we ourselves might be able to bring to bear for the purpose at once of defending ourselves and of putting heart into the Siamese...".[20] He further reiterated in August that Thailand sought to compromise with the "highest bidder"

---

[20] M. Coultas (B), 16 May 1939, F5250. See also minuted by M.J.R. Talbout in Foreign Office minutes, 21 June 1939, F6310.

and any inaction could be detrimental to British.[21] Unfortunately, his call for aid was rejected as Britain they had their hands tied in Europe and lacked both the will and power to fend off Japanese advancement in Asia. Exhausting their options for Western assistance, Phibun realized that the best option to prevent a bloodbath and complete occupation of their country, was to side with the Japanese.

December 8, 1941 at 2:00am, less than two hours after the attack on Pearl Harbor, the Japanese landed on the shores of southern Thailand.[22] There was a void in military and police commandment in Bangkok as Phibun was in an inspection mission in eastern Thailand. In his place was Adun Adhundecharat, the Bangkok Police General and Deputy Prime Minister and Foreign Minister Direk Jayanama, who were not delegated power to make immediate decisions in response to this advancement. The second wave of Japanese forces landed along the Kra Isthmus, near the provinces of Chumphon and Prachuap Khiri Khan.[23] Whether Phibun's absence was a coincidence or entirely intentional to postpone Japanese demands, continues to draw speculation today.

Five hours after the first landing, Phibun rushed back to Bangkok for the government Cabinet meeting. The

---

[21] Crosby to FO, 3 August 1939, F10131.
[22] U.S. Department of the Army, *Thailand Operations Record, Japanese Monograph #177* (Tokyo: Headquarters Army Forces Far East, 1953), 4-7.
[23] Thawi Bunyaket, *Thailand and World War II* (*ไทยกับสงครามโลกครั้งที่ 2*), (Bangkok: Sripanya Press, 1966), 174, appendix to Direk Jayanama's (ดิเรก ชัยนาม) book of the same name.

Cabinet had been arguing about the Japanese presence as well as the best course of action to protect Thai sovereignty. Amidst a room of senior level officials, Adun Adhundecharat held firm on the stance to follow through with Japanese demands, echoing earlier sentiments that continuously fighting would only result in a hopeless and costly military battle.[24] The imagery that Adun presented was an Imperial Japanese Army that had overwhelming military potential to easily crush Thailand as seen through their successful campaigns in the Philippines and Malaya. By noon, Phibun called for a ceasefire for the sake of negotiating with the Japanese. Looking back on this decision, Retired Air Chief Marshal Thawi Chunlasap—who years later became a major player in the resistance movement and eventually a powerful figure in Thai politics—noted that by permitting Japanese passage into Thailand, the country prevented the utter destruction and control of their country.[25] This reality and the story of the sacrifice of southern Thais to defend the occupation of their homeland would come to be used during post-war negotiations.

On December 9, 1941, an agreement was reached between Thailand and Japan. The following provisions were summarized by Thawi Bunyakeyt:[26]

---

[24] Ibid.
[25] Ibid.
[26] John B. Haseman, *The Thai Resistance Movement During World War II* (Chiang Mai: Silkworm Books, 2002), 46, as cited in Bunyaket, (1966), 174.

1. *The Thai government **permitted** Japan to send troops through Thailand to other countries in the region, notably, Malaya and Burma.*
2. *The Japanese troops would not disarm Thai forces.*
3. *Japanese forces would only pass through, not remain in, Bangkok.*
4. *The agreement was the only military in nature and did not imply a political or military alliance. No further requirements were to be levied on Thailand.*

Attention should be drawn to Thailand's use of the word *'permit'* (อนุญาติ). The choice to use the word placed limitations on Japanese military activities and would go on to serve as a point of appeal during the Nuremberg Trial to highlight the country's dire circumstances leading up to the alliance and its choice to *'permit'* rather than agree to or approve of Japanese passage. In response to the agreement, on December 21st, Japanese invasion forces moved out of the country to regroup and restrategize in Malaya.

The partnership with Thailand offered several advantages to the Japanese. The first reason was Thailand's geological positioning. As Thailand has access to both land and sea passages into British Malaya, the country would serve as the main launching pad for a successful southern invasion. The Japanese also believed that Thailand could serve as a critical supply base for its campaign into Burma. Such logistical and administrative advantages could lead to a successful conquest of India in later years. The second reason was rooted in economics. As

Japan struggled with debt accumulated from campaigns in China and Manchuria, Thailand's surplus rice exports could prove a valuable asset to continue to fund the Japanese war effort.[27] Finally, as Thailand was never colonized by western powers, Japan sought saw its partnership with Thailand advantageous in justifying and promoting its Greater East Asia Co-Prosperity Sphere ideology. Thailand could serve as the epitome of what a nation free from Western colonialism—under Japanese leadership, indubitably—would look like.

On January 25, 1942, Bangkok declared war on the United States and the United Kingdom. Under Thai law, all members of the Council of Regents were required to sign laws and declarations issued in the name of the King. Pridi refused to sign the declaration, noting that Parliament had not been consulted on the decision and thus the act was deemed illegal. Shortly after, he proceeded to go into hiding.[28] The declaration was returned to Phibun with only two signatures. In response to the declaration, the British declared war on Thailand and deemed the country an enemy of the state. On the opposite end, Thai minister M.R. Seni Pramoj refused to give the war declaration to Secretary of State Cordell Hull[29], an act that was deemed "one of the most dramatic causes of the continued American friendship for Thailand".[30]

---

[27] Haseman, 1.

[28] Manich Jumsai, *History of Anglo-Thai Relations* (Bangkok: Chalermnit Press, 1970), 261.

[29] Quaritch-Wales, "Thailand-Key to the Coming Attack on Japan,": 259.

[30] Haseman, *The Thai Resistance Movement During World War II*, 22.

These realities and reactions would go on to define two Allied countries' approaches to post-war negotiations for Thailand and further highlight the "differences of interest the two allies had in Asia".[31]

While analyzing the decisions made prior to the Thai-Japanese alliance as well as through concluding the findings above, it is notable that Thailand's decisions underwent extensive planning and consideration. Understanding the Allies' lack of ability to provide assistance, Phibun refused to allow Thailand to fall into Japanese hands and instead opted to negotiate a deal to permit free passage. Phibun decision during this time was reevaluated by Mom Rajawongse Seni Pramoj's (หม่อมราชวงศ์เสนีย์ ปราโมช) during his statement to the U.S. State Department, in which he stated:

> *Before I left Bangkok on my mission to this country... I asked the Prime Minister point-blank to tell me what was the foreign policy of Thailand. Were we pro-Japanese, pro-English, pro-American or pro-anything? He replied that we were no pro any other country in particular. We were pro-Thai.*[32]

Under military and political pressure from Japan, Thailand had officially entered the war. Japan saw their "alliance" with Thailand as one of its many successes in cul-

---

[31] Bob Bergin, "OSS and Free Thai Operations in World War II," *Studies in Intelligence*, Vol. 55, No. 4 (2011): 12.

[32] James V. Martin "Thai-American Relations in World War II," *The Journal of Asian Studies* Volume 22, No.4, (1963): 451-467.

tivating Asian solidarity and towards their creation of a Greater East Asian Co-prosperity Sphere. The United States and Great Britain were now facing an even more prominent and stronger Axis presence in Asia. Especially in Britain's case, the Japanese presence in Thailand threatened their stronghold in Burma. Finally, Phibun and his administration were content with the fact that they acted in accordance with the circumstances presented to them. Little did Phibun, Japan, and the Allies know, was that the first attempt to organize an underground resistance was made seconds after the war declaration had been made.

Chapter Three

The Political, Economic, and Societal Impact of Phibun's Domestic and International Policies

While the underground movement underwent initial steps to establish communication with the West, the effects of the Phibun government's alliance with the Japanese began to take hold. Phibun moved to consolidate his power, pursuing militant nationalistic policies that sought to unify and civilize Thai society and culture. Such *Thaification* laws led to the discrimination and containment of Chinese and Muslim Thais, as well as other tribal and ethnic minorities, who Phibun argued, were failing to assimilate to Thai culture. On the international front, Japan moved captured POWs into the western province of Kanchanaburi. There, they would spend the next years of their lives slaving away to the construction of what would be nicknamed 'Death Railroad'.

Domestic Policies: The Concept and Implementation of Thaification

Between 1939 and 1942, Phibun enacted a series of cultural mandates called the 'state edicts of Thai society' (รัฐนิยม). These edicts focused on defining and standardizing what it meant to be 'civilized' Thai individuals. On top of providing Thais with a 'template' on how to become the idealized Thai citizen, Phibun's justification for the edicts were both for the sake of "strengthen[ing] Siam in the context of a global war" as well as to prove its status as a strong and resilient state through its ability to "remake the nation and its culture from above".[1] The mandates were separated into five major themes; nationalism, assimilation, unity, progress, and national security.

The first edict, issued on June 24, 1939, officially changed the country's name from Siam to Thailand, arguing that the country name should reflect the Thai race. The second theme involved assimilation. For the Phibun administration, this meant applying pressures and facilitation for ethnic minorities and non-Thai speaking individuals to *prove* their membership in the Thai national community. In this sense, all Thais were required to speak, write, and read the central Thai dialect and avoid using local or ethnic vernacular. An edict was also included a requirement to honor the flag and national anthem by-the-hour. By 1942, a National Culture Commission was created to define, disseminate, and

---

[1] Chris Baker and Pasuk Phongpaichit, *A History of Thailand* (Cambridge: Cambridge University Press, 2014), 131.

Chapter 3: The Impact of Phibun's Domestic and International Policies

moralize Thai culture.² The third theme involved unity, and distinctions between those from the 'northeastern', 'southern', or other areas were no longer described or used. Popular songs that sang to the distinction of different communities were either banned or had words censored for the sake of reimagining Thais as a single, homogeneous entity. The fourth theme was progressed, which focused on becoming self-reliant as well as incentives to buy and invest in Thai goods. Edicts also defined what was the proper Thai dress code, etiquette, and social way of life. The last theme revolved around national security. Government-sponsored radio programs that broadcast news or slogans to help identify what activities can be deemed "treasonous and anti-national" and the punishments that would entail.

Interestingly, in 1944, the Phibun administration released a 14-point Code of National Bravery, a code of conduct that mirrored the Japanese Bushido Code. The code spoke to the Thai people's unconditional love for their nation, their ability to sacrifice themselves to protect their nation, and the essence of being Thai, which included loyalty to their leader, their Buddhist faith, self-sufficiency, ambitious nature, and peace-loving yet martial mentality.³ In Phibun's own view, the edicts and the role of the government itself are to 'reform and reconstruct the various aspects of society, especially its culture, which here signifies growth and beauty, orderliness, progress and

---

² Ibid., 131-132.
³ Ibid., 134.

uniformity, and the morality of the nation'".[4]

Phibun and his administration also moved to push for economic nationalism. These policies, in particular, took a toll on the ethnic Chinese population and such Anti-Chinese sentiment on the economic front was a result of two elements. The first was the growing realization that large amounts of money were being remitted back to China by Chinese Thais, constituting a substantial drain on the Thai economy.[5] The second element was in relation to the growing anti-Japanese movement in Chinese Thai communities. Beginning during the 1937 Sino-Japanese War, Chinese Thai communities organized a series of boycotts against Japanese goods. As Japan had gradually become a major trading partner to Thailand after the signing of the 1941 Free Passage declaration, Phibun and his administration believed that the boycotts would harm the Thai economy and threaten foreign relations. In response, Phibun's government took over Chinese-run businesses. New or renewed contracts would then go to ethnic Thais or ethnic Chinese businessmen who were close to the administration.[6] Other restrictions and systematic discrimination experienced by ethnic Chinese were unfair taxes, limited job opportunities, Chinese school closures, the abolishment

---

[4] Kobkua Suwannathat-Pian, *Thailand's Durable Premier: Phibun through Three Decades, 1932–1957* (Kuala Lumpur: Oxford University Press, 1995), 102.

[5] David K. Wyatt, *Thailand: A Short History* (New Haven: Yale University Press, 2003), 254.

[6] Anne Booth, *Colonial Legacies: Economic and Social Development in East and Southeast Asia* (University of Hawaii Press 2007), 122.

Chapter 3: THE IMPACT OF PHIBUN'S DOMESTIC AND INTERNATIONAL POLICIES

of Chinese newspapers, and an unfair annual alien registration fee.[7] In the end, during the duration of the was ethnic Chinese in Thailand became what E. Bruce Reynolds coins "international orphans"—individuals who lacked political and economic support from a country they deemed their home (Thailand) and were now cut off from their mainland network (China).[8]

Lastly, the most impactful and consequential domestic policy to ever come out of the Phibun administration is the consolidation of political power in the Thai military. Since the 1932 coup and Phibun's rise to power in the following years, the Thai military adopted substantial control over the national government. Rising to the self-proclaimed title of 'phu nam' (leader, ผู้นำ), Phibun promoted himself to major general ad adopted other titles including foreign minister, commander-in-chief of the army, defense minister, and even rector at the country's top university.[9] Furthermore, he approved legislation that postponed democratic transition for another ten years, preserving the seats and ranks of non-elected officials as well as spearheaded expansionist activities to reclaim formerly lost territories in Laos and Cambodia.[10]

---

[7] Wyatt, 254.

[8] E. Bruce Reynolds, "'International Orphans: The Chinese in Thailand during World War II'," *Journal of Southeast Asian Studies*, Vol. 28, No. 2 (1997), 365-388.

[9] E. Bruce Reynolds, "Phibun Songkhram and Thai Nationalism in the Fascist Era," *European Journal of East Asian Studies*, Volume 3. (2004): 117.

[10] Ibid.

On top of centralizing his power, he had built a cult of personality around himself, advertising his images throughout the country, from billboards to newspapers. Slogans like 'One nation, Thailand, one nation, Phibun Songkhram, one aim, victory' and 'Our Nation's Security Depends on Believing in Our Leader' as well as topics that spoke to irredentism to military exceptionalism were constantly blasted over the radio.[11] Military conscription and training for adolescent boys were also established, beginning as early as during middle school with the Boy Scouts and Junior Red Cross. Phibun's centralization of power in Bangkok was especially detrimental to sub-national territories, especially in the indigenous or ethnic Malay Muslim areas, who were now deprived of their ability to determine their local laws, attend religious school and services, and elect provincial representatives.[12] These actions would later lead to the issue of ethnic fractionalization, prolonged conflict, and violence in Thailand's Deep South for years to come.

International Policies: The Birth of the Siamese-Burma Railroad

The Japanese position in the Pacific was beginning to waver. After their loss at the hands of the British in the

---

[11] Thamsook Numnonda, *Thailand and the Japanese Presence, 1941-45*. (Singapore: ISEAS Publishing, 1977), 29.

[12] Arnaud Dubus and Sor Rattanamanee Polkla, *Policies of the Thai state towards the Malay Muslim South (1978-2010)* (OpenEdition Books, 2011), 13.

Battle of Midway and the Battle of the Coral Sea in 1942, passages to the Andaman Sea and the Bay of Bengal were now occupied by Allied forces. Japan now needed an alternative supply route to sustain a successful campaign in Burma. They turned towards mainland Thailand.

The Japanese Imperial Army planned to build a rail line in Southeast Asia was conceived as early as 1939. Though building a railway connecting Thailand and Burma was one of the first concepts considered, efforts were abandoned as a construction through dense jungles, rugged mountains, and turbulent rivers proved to be extremely difficult. By mid-1942, the Imperial Japanese Army found a solution to such an impasse; it would be using its 61,000 captured POWs and 300,000 Asian

Australia's 8th Division disembarking into Singapore. Troop members either died defending posts in Malaya and Singapore or died in captivity working as POWs on the Thai-Burmas Railway.
Source: Wikimedia Commons

workers, as its main labor force. Ignoring the Geneva Protocol that forbids using POWs for forced labor, degradation, or punishment, Japan gathered captured Allied POWs from Singapore and Indonesian prison camps and immediately put them to work.

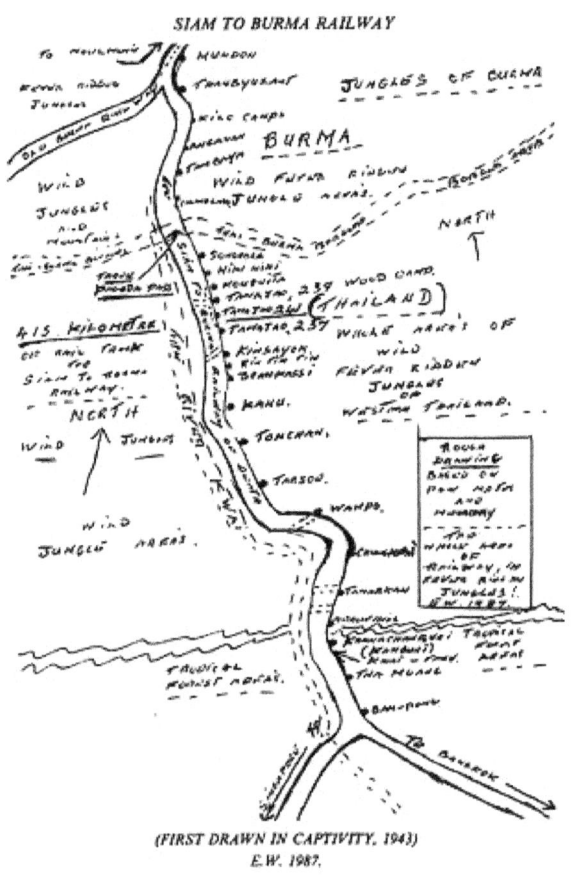

Map of the Prisoner of War Camps along the Thailand-Burma Railway drawn in captivity by Ernest Warwick.
Source: Wikimedia Commons

Chapter 3: THE IMPACT OF PHIBUN'S DOMESTIC AND INTERNATIONAL POLICIES

The Construction of the Thai-Burma Railway

Although officially known as the Thai-Burma Railway or the Siam-Bumas Railway, the nickname "Death Railway" was adopted due to the terribly high number of POWs and Asian laborers who died constructing the war-time infrastructure. Though records vary, approximately 14,000 Allied POWs and 90,000 Asian laborers lost their lives either due to horrific work conditions, starvation, vitamin deficiency, malaria, or dengue fever.[13] While the British were amongst the highest number of Allied POWs deaths at 6,904 soldiers, it was the Australian forces that were disproportionately affected. While 4,000 Australians were captured by German and Ottoman forces in Europe during World War I, more than 22,000 Australians were captured by the Japanese in the Asia-Pacific region. More than a third of Australian POWs lost their lives in captivity, totaling 20% of all Australian deaths during World War II.[14]

Asian Laborers, known in Japanese as romusha (労務者), consisted of people from Burma, Thailand, China, and Indonesia as well as individuals from Tamil, Java, and Karen tribal communities. Due to its proximately to Thailand, the largest romusha percentage came from Burma and Malaya, with estimates amounting to 90,000

---

[13] Australian Government Department of Veteran Affairs, "The Burma--Thailand Railway and Hellfire Pass," Anzac Centenary Program, https://anzacportal.dva.gov.au/history/conflicts/thaiburma-railway-and-hellfire-pass (accessed Dec 18, 2018).

[14] Rod Beattie, *The Death Railway: A Brief History of the Thailand-Burma Railway* (Image Makers Co., Ltd, 2005), 10.

and 75,000 individuals respectively. In total, Japan had over 200,000 romushas at their disposal.[15] Japanese recruitment for romusha initially began as paid contracts, with additional compensation in the form of food, clothing, housing. However, after experiencing the physical and mental fatigue of building rail lines through uncharted terrain as well as the gradual reduction of monetary compensation from the Japanese Army, contractors began fleeing after their expiration dates. Fearing that the decrease of romusha would slow down construction, Japan changed its tactic to forced conscription. Unlike Allied POWs, romushas did not possess either military or educational backgrounds and as such were not as physically conditioned or informed of oncoming health hazards. Furthermore, due to their large numbers, romusha camps became extremely crowded, prompting unsanitary conditions that produced high rates of illnesses and infection. Approximately 90,000 romushas lives were lost by the end of the construction period, averaging to about 360 persons per mile of track laid on the Death Railroad.[16]

Contrary to their Allied counterparts whose government continuously worked towards repatriation, romusha had difficulty returning to their country or place of origin. Despite comprising of the largest workforce

---

[15] Australian Government Department of Veteran Affairs, "Rŏmusha Recruitment," Anzac Centenary Program,
https://anzacportal.dva.gov.au/history/conflicts/burma-thailand-railway-and-hellfire-pass/burma-thailand-railway-and-hellfire-2 (accessed Dec 18, 2018).
[16] Ibid.

Chapter 3: THE IMPACT OF PHIBUN'S DOMESTIC AND INTERNATIONAL POLICIES

and experiencing the highest death toll, romusha did not obtain the same international recognition for their suffering, resulting in them wandering aimlessly in Thailand or starting a new life in different parts of the Pacific. Those who did return home were unable to leave the country until many years after the end of the war. As many romusha were illiterate and incapable of documenting their personal accounts via writing, the history and experiences of this large Asian workforce continue to remain in the shadows of World War II.

The highest death count occurred towards the end of the construction period in 1943. With the continual torture and mistreatment of POWs as well as unfavorable camp conditions brought by the monsoon season, death rates had reached over 20% of the total workforce.

Australian and Dutch prisoners of war in the Tarsau camp in Thailand. The soldiers are experiencing vitamin B1 deficiency (known as beriberi). Source: Wikimedia Commons

A drawing depicting the conditions of a POW camp, with the center subject being a severely malnourished man staring at a cholera victim laying on a bamboo stretcher.
Source: The Imperial War Museum

POWs witnessed an uptick in cruel and gruesome physical punishment as the Japanese Army rushed the construction of the railway. With pressures from Tokyo to continue their campaign into Burma and eventually India before the British were able to regroup, the Imperial Army forced the romusha and POWs to enter a period known as 'The Speedo', a Japanese transliteration of the word

Chapter 3: The Impact of Phibun's Domestic and International Policies

'Speed'. While a prisoner might have been expected to work ten-hour days and drill a meter into mountainsides, soon increased to fifteen then eighteen-hour days and three meters of drilling. Workers who were deemed slow or who failed to meet the day's goal were subjected to inhumane acts of abuse, including beatings, torture, isolation, verbal degradation, and starvation.

When rail lines were unable to be built around mountains, cuttings[17] were required to continue the rail track. One of the most difficult and longest of these cuttings was Hellfire Pass (ช่องเขาขาด). With the implementation of 'Speedo', forced laborers were required to work throughout the night, having only the light from oil lamps to guide their path. The loud noises, dark atmosphere, and shadows of tired prisoners reflected on mountainsides reminded the POWs of popular depictions of hell, and the name Hellfire Pass eventually stuck. Excavation of the railway cutting was done mostly by hand, and by the time of its completion, it was 75 meters (246 feet) in length and 25 meters (82 feet) in depth. At its completion, the entire railroad measured 415 kilometers (about 257 miles), beginning at Nong Pladuk, Thailand and ending at Thanbyuzayat, Burma.

The memories and history of the Death Railroad continue to live on in Thailand. The Thailand Burma Railway Centre Museum in Kanchanaburi Province contains photographs, images, and blurbs of the horrors behind

---

[17] Cuttings were the mechanical excavation and removal of rock material via digging or drilling.

Hellfire Pass Entrance decorated with Australian flags and other offerings in remembrance of the lives lost.
Source: Wikimedia Commons

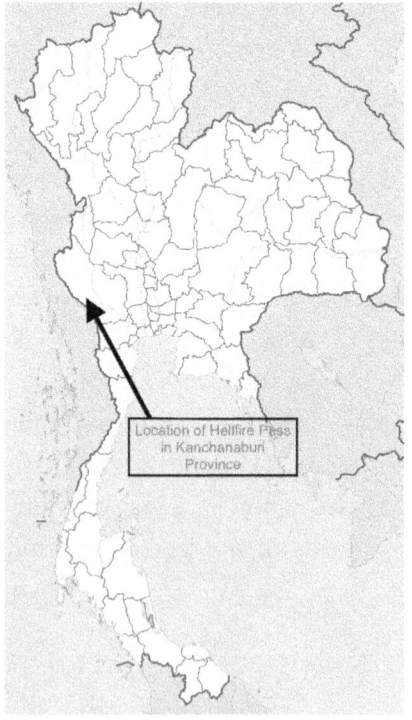

Map of Thailand with the location of the Hellfire Pass cutting.
Source: Wikimedia Commons

the railroad's construction, while also searching as an ongoing research facility. The museum continues to build its database of past prisoners, including some 105,000 profiles of Allied POWs. The museum, managed and curated by Ron Beattie, also sponsors personalized, annual trips for relatives of those who worked to build the rail line, taking them as far as the border of Burma.

*(Left) Entrance to the Thailand Burma Railway Centre. (Right) The start of the Thai-Burma Railway Line in Mawlamyine, Burma.
Source: Wikimedia Commons*

Across from the museum is the Kanchanaburi War Cemetery, where the bodies of some 6,900 Dutch, Australian, and British POWs are buried. Various books have contributed substantially to expanding the history of those who struggled and lost their lives constructing the railway, including but not limited to: John Coast's *Railroad of Death* (1947), Gavin Daws' *Prisoners of the Japanese: POWs of World War II in the Pacific War* (1994), Leslie Hall's *The Blue Haze* (1996), and Roy H. Whitecross' *Slaves of the Son of Heaven: The Personal Story of an Australian Prisoner of the Japanese During the*

Years 1942 to 1945 (1951).[18] Movies such as 1957's *The Bridge Over River Kwai* and 2013's *The Railway Man* also helped memorialize the stories POWs and bring them to an international audience. While only parts of the railroad exist today due to bombings, reforestation, and demolition from the Allied side to pay for reparations, parts of the rail from between Nong Pladuk and Nam Tok was reopened in 1957 to serve as transportation for the local community. In particular, the bridge and train route over the Mae Klong 'Khwae Yai River' River (commonly known as the River Kwai) remains a popular tourist attraction.

---

[18] For a list of recommended reading on the Thai-Burma Railway, please visit the Australian Government's Department of Veterans' Affairs Anzac Portal: https://anzacportal.dva.gov.au/bibliography.

Chapter Four

The Free Thai Resistance Movement

"The situation in Siam was different from any that had ever confronted OSS in an enemy-occupied country. Instead of a resistance movement, such as was encountered in European countries, there existed in Siam what might best be described as a patriotic governmental conspiracy against the Japanese in which most of the key figures of the state were involved."[1]

—Kermit Roosevelt

The Birth of the X.O. Group

An organized resistance against the Japanese began well before the Thai-Japanese alliance. One of the first series of meetings took place on December 11, 1941, in Pridi's

---

[1] Bergin, "OSS and Free Thai Operations in World War II," 11.

home.² Those in attendance comprised of a handful of civilian leaders previously part of the 1932 coup d'etat as well as elder, Thai autocrats. Topics of discussion in the initial meeting included the opposition of Phibun's policies, anti-Japanese sentiments, and plans to establish a government-in-exile. This core, inner circle of leadership called themselves the X.O. Group.

Member of the inner circle of the X.O. were comprised of the following: Foreign Minister Direk Jayanama (ดิเรก ชัยนาม), soon to be sent to Tokyo for espionage missions as the Thai Ambassador to Japan; National Assembly and chairman of the Tobacco Monopoly in the Ministry of Finance, Sa-nguan Tularak (สงวน ตุลารักษ์); Rear Admiral Sangwon Yuthakit (หลวงสังวรยุทธกิจ), the deputy commander of the Royal Thai Navy who also possessed jurisdiction over the capital's military police; and long-time Pridi confidantes Luang Kri Dechati-wong (หม่อมหลวงกรี เดชาติวงศ์), Charun Subsaeng (จรูญ สืบแสง), Thongplao Chonaphum (ทองเปลว ชลภูมิ), and Thawi Tawetikun (ทวี ตะเวทิกุล).

Weighing several options, the group eventually developed a four-step plan that would form the basis of their resistance movement; (1) reduce the power and influence of Phibun's government and its policies with Japan, (2) disrupt and incapacitate Japanese operations through either reconnaissance missions or confrontational engagements, (3) launch propaganda that would

---

² Malai Chumpanit (มาลัย ชูพินิจ) (pseudonym Chanthana 'นายฉันหนา') X.O. Group เรื่องภายในขบวนเสรีไทย, (Thai Panit Publications, 1964), 25.

promote the dissention between Phibun and the Japanese, and, (4) establish contact with the Allies.[3] These goals epitomized both *internal (ภายนอกประเทศ)* and *external (ภายในประเทศ)* resistance activities, interacting with each other interchangeably to complement and ensure the success of the other. A clear case example of the X.O. group's internal and external resistance mission was the successful exfiltration of U.S. soldiers under Japanese captivity through back and forth U.S.-Thai transmission (external) and on-the-ground coordination in deceiving the Japanese for the POW's release (internal). This unique style of reconnaissance would go on to legitimize the Seri Thai as a resistance coalition as well as an important source of military intelligence for the Allied powers.

One of the first goals of the Seri Thai was to increase and consolidate its membership. After the signing of the Japanese Free Passage Treaty, isolated attacks and protests against Japanese presence gradually increased. Such attacks began drawing the suspicion of Phibun and the Japanese, with the most famous incident being a failed effort to dynamite the Lampang-Chiang Mai tunnel.[4] Wishing to maintain the secrecy of an anti-Japanese resistance force as well as consolidate the movement's goals, Pridi sought to incorporate these smaller groups into the larger Free Thai Movement. Pridi, as well as other members of the X.O. group, began recruiting close allies, acquiring people from the police, civil services, and other areas of

---

[3] Chumpanit, 72-73.
[4] Margaret Landon, "Thailand Under the Japanese." *Asia and the Americas*, Issue 44.9 (1944), 389.

the formal Thai infrastructure. This included Chamkat Phalangkun (จำกัด พลางกูร), head of the Thai liberation movement Ku Chat (กู้ชาติ), who merged his organization with the Free Thai bringing with him high ranking officials Chamlong Daorueng, Komet Khrueatrachu, Yon Somanon, and Thawin Udon. These men would go on to command guerilla activities and reconnaissance missions in Northeastern Thailand and China.[5] Chamkat himself would also soon play a major role in recruiting other resistance groups into the Free Thai Movement. With the initial foundation for internal resistance organized, efforts were made towards external resistance—establishing contact and partnership with Allied forces.

Establishing Communication: Risk-Taking, Gridlocks, and A Lot of Miscommunication

One could say that the foundation for U.S.-Seri Thai partnership began with M.R. Seni Pramoj's refusal to deliver Thailand's declaration of war to the Secretary of State. This event unfolded in a dramatic, somewhat Oscar-worthy performance. Tapping on his coat while looking Secretary Hull in the eye, M.R. Seni stated, "I'm keeping the declaration in my pocket because I am convinced it does not represent the will of the Thai people. With American help, I propose to prove it".[6] The decla-

---

[5] Chuphanit, 66-69.
[6] Walter Fitzmaurice, "Thailand, Ally in Secret, Snooped under Japs' Noses", *Newsweek*, 3. 9. 1945, 26.

ration of war was never delivered to Secretary Hull and in response, the U.S. never declared war against Thailand. Speaking to a symposium several years after the conclusion of the war, M.R. Seni stated:

> "During the War, the United States proved to be our best friend, helping us when we had fallen to the worst, at which time we could not foresee a dim of light of independence. The relationship between Thailand and the United States of America during these days was tied up so tightly that I can hardly be broken up... our Embassy... decided not to observe the Thai government surrender to the Japanese... and to... organize resistance against the Japanese, believing that all Thai would help one another to regain independence from the Japanese".[7]

M.R. Seni took swift actions on his proposal. He requested assistance from the United States, including the funding to train Thai students and expatriates to oppose the Japanese by force, establishing communication with mainland Thailand, and permission to carry secret activities with other countries for the sake of aiding the Thai effort.[8] Furthermore, M.R. Seni presented his manifesto of purpose and goals, presenting six points to the U.S.:[9]

---

[7] M.R. Seni Praoj, manuscript of a speech given 17 August 1946, unpaged. (Excerpt taken from Hasemen, 2002)
[8] Haseman, 23.
[9] Nai Samrej, "That Thailand May Be Free," *Asia and the Americas*, (February 1945), 94-95.

1. The Seri Thai was not a political party but an organization whose main objective was to restore Thailand's independence.
2. The Japanese army was the enemy of the Thai because their armed forces had invaded Thailand.
3. The Bangkok government was a puppet government because it had cooperated with the enemy against the will of the people.
4. The Seri Thai regarded itself as the representative agency representing the will of the Thai people everywhere.
5. The Seri Thai would not interfere with the law of succession of the king.
6. A constitutional government and democracy would be restored to Thailand after the country's freedom was restored. The Seri Thai would release all political prisoners and would organize a People's Court to investigate those who had cooperated with the enemy.

Both the requests and the manifesto were successively approved and recognized by the U.S. American support for Free Thai (เสรีไทย), a name coined by M.R. Seni for the newly founded organization, solidified on April 1942 under the aegis of the Office of Strategic Services (OSS).

Resistance efforts in Great Britain compared to the U.S. were complicated and extremely challenging. Despite an equal number of students expatriates showing opposition to the Phibun administration, resistance organizations had a difficult time convincing the British government to assist. This was due to several factors, from geographic isolation to factionalism as well as the absence of a prominent, central figure that could propel the resistance movement forward. In addition, there was no doubt that Britain's lingering feelings of betrayal after the Thai war declaration slowed the process of the resistance coalition.

Eventually, a strong cadre of Thai leaders emerged in London. One of the leaders, Sano Tanbunyeun, contacted M.R. Seni in Washington D.C. and asked for his assistance in covering the British government to support the resistance movement. As M.R. Seni was preoccupied in the U.S., he sent League of Nations representative, Mani Sanasen. Alongside Sano, Mani directed all Thai efforts in Britain with the former coordinating student resistance efforts and the latter acting and M.R. Seni's representative in England.[10]

The growth of pro-Allied Thai students attracted the attention of the Special Operations Executive (SOE), Britain's clandestine warfare organization and the OSS' counterpart. The SOE had recognized the potential of a resistance effort through their interaction with Prince Suphasawatwongsanit Sawatdiwat ('Prince Suphasawa'), who also served as Chief of Palace Security. The Prince, along with his sister Queen Ramphai Phanni (widow of exiled King Prajadhipok) and Prince Chula Chakraphong (grandson of the late King Chulalongkorn), was sympathetic to the Allied-student protests.

---

[10] Haseman, *The Thai Resistance Movement During World War II*, 27.

Having been contacted by resistance leaders Sena Tambunyen and Puey Ungphakorn in early March 1942, Prince Suphasawa utilized his high-level status to contact Churchill's office.[11] He proposed the idea of having Thai volunteers infiltrate the mainland and took the initiative in writing and submitting a plan detailing operation opportunities to weaken Japan forces.[12] In response, the SOE assumed responsibilities for the implementation of British-Thai reconnaissance missions and by late June, approval was received to utilize Thai volunteers.

The Free Thai in the U.S. and Britain moved forward to establish communication with mainland Thailand to notify them of their existence and their partnership with Allied forces. These initial efforts were proven difficult. Wary of potential interception from both Phibun and the Japanese forces, the resistance coalition in the U.S. and Britain agreed that the best way to communicate with Seri Thai members in Thailand was to send high-ranking officials into China. These officials would then make their way to Bangkok on foot through the jungles of Vietnam or Laos. Similarly, Seri Thai members were to travel to China to deliver messages from the X.O. group to Seri Thai members in Britain and the United States. Both the OSS and SOE soon realized that this method was highly scrutinized by the Chinese Intelligence Chief, General Tai Lai.

---

[11] E. Bruce Reynolds, *Thailand's Secret War: OSS, SOE and the Free Thai Underground During World War II* (Cambridge: Cambridge University Press, 2010), 25.

[12] Wanthani, ed., *Neung Satawan Suphasawat*, (Bangkok, 2000), 61, and Suphasawat to Seni, 14 May 1942, FO 371-31862-3953, PRO.

Chapter 4: THE FREE THAI RESISTANCE MOVEMENT

With the passing of Joint Chief of Staff Directive 245 (JCS 245), all U.S. commutative operations from China were conducted under the control of the Sino-American Co-operative Organization (SACO). Based in Chungking, China, SACO was comprised of both American and Chinese intelligence officers, with the former serving under Navy Captain Milton Miles, and the latter under General Tai Lai. Strict, unyielding, and difficult, Tai Lai "held absolute control of operations directed into Thailand and also over the dissemination of much of the intelligence collected on Southeast Asia.[13] Despite SACO's presence as a mutual intelligence gathering entity, it was Tai Lai that was responsible for approving all communication efforts and clandestine operations from China into Thailand.

Many Thai officials who arrived in China saw themselves being blocked with Chinese bureaucratic impasses. Chamkat, for example, noticed that the letters and telegrams he sent to his colleagues abroad failed to be forwarded in a timely manner, were missing, or deemed undeliverable.[14] In addition, other Seri Thai agents saw their missions severely delayed, resulting in deaths due to weather conditions, unpreparedness, or logistical oversight.[15] Frustrated with these administrative impasses, Chamkat wrote a final report, beginning with a call to Allied support for Thailand. The report then detailed the opposition to Phibun's government including his administration's current wartime policies. Chamkat fur-

---

[13] Haseman, *The Thai Resistance Movement During World War II*, 34.
[14] Haseman, 46.
[15] Reynolds, *Thailand's Secret War*, 45.

ther expanded on details involving the formation and organization of the Thai resistance group and the X.O. group itself, listing out their current activities and projected plans for stymieing Japanese influence in the country. This report would later turn out to become the Allies' first written account of an existing Thai resistance movement in the U.S. and Britain.[16] Unfortunately, Chamkat was unable to see his efforts come to fruition as he died shortly after on October 7, 1943. While stomach cancer was the accepted reasoning for his sudden passing, others have argued the possibility of foul play, specifically poisoning by either Chinese vigilantes or Japanese spies.[17]

Though the resistance lost one of its most crucial leaders, these series of events culminated in a variety of changes in the Allied communications strategy. Chamkat's death spurred the U.S. to slowly reduce its interaction with SACO and move its communications group out of Southeast China and into Sri Lanka, successfully establishing continuous, reciprocal contact between themselves and the Free Thai movement. With communications finally in place, the resistance movement set off to reclaim their country.

---

[16] Ibid., 46.

[17] Professor Piset Noraniti Seetabut (ศาสตราจารย์พิเศษ นรนิติ เศรษฐบุตร) "(Chamkat Phalangkun) จำกัด พลางกูร,", King Prajadhipok Institute, 2016. https://tinyurl.com/yynzb862. (accessed July 2, 2019)

Chapter 4: THE FREE THAI RESISTANCE MOVEMENT

Mission Successes of the Free Thai

The underground Thai movement contributed significantly to the Allied war effort in Southeast Asia. As mentioned briefly at the beginning of this chapter, the Free Thai's unique model of an interchanging, two-pronged reconnaissance approach contributed greatly to the U.S. war effort in Southeast Asia. Over 50,000 Thai Volunteers underwent excruciating training and dangerous missions and treks to collect and report findings to U.S. and British supporters stationed in China and other areas of Indochina. While some made it back to their designated bases to report on the Japanese Army's location, others were either captured, killed, or had disappeared. The Thai nationals were walking on thin ice in their homeland.

In Phrae Province, Pridi Panomyong and Thong Kantatham led and launched parachuting operations to sneak in Allied forces for reconnaissance missions. The most notable ones were *Operation Hotfoot* and *Operation Numeral*, operations that helped deploy weapons, supplies, and medicine to supporting troop members either in Thailand or conflict areas in Southeast Asia.[18] The lives of Thai volunteers were constantly endangered, having to navigate around Allied bombing campaigns, rescuing fallen foreign soldiers, avoiding Japanese detection, all while broadcasting findings and weather reports to partners in the U.S.

---

[18] Bob Bergin, "OSS and Free Thai Operations in World War II," *Studies in Intelligence*, Vol. 55, No. 4 (2011): 10-20.

Arguably, one of the most fascinating exfiltration missions during World War II was the search and rescue of Flying Tiger pilot, William McGarry. On May 22, 1942, at his headquarters in Kunming China, General Claire L. Chennault called for a meeting with his American Volunteer Group the "Flying Tigers". Chennault wished to launch a surprise attack against the Japanese Air Force in northern Thailand, who at the time, was busy ambushing Britain's RAF (Royal Air Force) Base in Eastern Burma. Chennault proposed that the P-40s (the designated fighter planes of the Flying Tigers) would fly from Kunming to Loiwing, China, refuel, and continue to fly towards the airstrip at Nam Sang in Burma. From there, the planes would be within close range of Chiang Mai, where they would stay overnight and strike early in the morning. General Chennault would not have predicted, however, that that would be the last time he saw one of his best pilots, William McGarry, for the next three years.

William "Black Mac" McGarry joined the Flying Tigers before the beginning of the U.S.'s involvement in the war in 1941. He first learned to pilot planes for the U.S. Army Air Forces at Selfridge Field (now known as Selfridge ANGB Airport), Michigan. With ten (10) successful missions under his belt, McGarry set off for the Chiang Mai mission on May 23, hoping to provide top cover for his four comrades.

On March 24, 1942, while flying over Chiang Mai to attack the Japanese Air Force, McGarry's plane was shot down by the anti-aircraft fire. Taking quick action after the attack, McGarry parachuted into a jungle clearing

Chapter 4: THE FREE THAI RESISTANCE MOVEMENT

American Volunteer Group the Flying Tigers standing in front of a P-40 Warhawk aircraft.
Source: Patrick Air Force Base

near the province of Mae Hong Son (approximately 230 kilometers/145 miles from Chiang Mai). After wandering the northern Thai jungles for three weeks, he was eventually found and apprehended by the Thai police patrolling the area. McGarry was quickly turned over to the Japanese military, who imprisoned him under a compound in Thammasat University, Bangkok. What the Japanese didn't know, however, that the compound was in the line of sight of Pridi.

Around the same time, communication between the Pridi's group and the Allied forces were well established. Seri Thai members reported on Japanese movement, important logistical bases, weaponry stock, and in this situation, the names of individuals imprisoned by the Japanese. Pridi, now back in the government in the capacity of a Regent[19] to the Thai King, presented himself in alliance with the Japanese for the sake of collecting information to channel to his Western Allies. Aware of McGarry's service as an American fighter pilot, Pridi moved to convince the Japanese that as Thai officials had effectively 'captured' him, McGarry should be deemed a Thai prisoner, albeit under Japanese oversight.

Hopes of McGarry's release began in 1944. In hopes of circumventing Tai Lai's assistance in infiltrating Seri Thai agents from China, Nicole Smith contacted Chennault asking for assistance in establishing a radio station and jump-off point for his agents.[20] As Chennault had recently built a new airstrip for his Volunteer Group near the Chinese-Laos border, he granted Smith permission to establish his radio station there. Once Smith's agents successfully arrived in Thailand, it was Chennault's turn to reach out for assistance.

Chennault asked Smith if he could have the Seri Thai investigate on the status of his AVG pilot. Within four days, Smith reported that McGarry was well and alive. McGarry was still kept inside the POW camp supervised by Thai police who served under General Adun Adundetcharat. A resistance member himself, Adun worked to keep POWs out of Japanese hands, all while coaching captured soldiers how to respond during Japanese inter-

---

[19] Thai Regents (ผู้สำเร็จราชการแทนพระองค์) work to execute the functions of the monarch during periods of incapacity or interregnum. In this case, Pridi served as Regent as King Ananda Mahidol was studying in Switzerland.

[20] Bergin, "OSS and Free Thai Operations in World War II," 17.

rogation. When asked if McGarry was well enough to attempt an escape, both McGarry and the Thai resistance members quickly confirmed.[21] When Pridi was made aware of McGarry's relation to Chennault and the Flying Tigers, he informed the two men that the Seri Thai coalition would do whatever they can to rescue McGarry and bring him home.

Removing McGarry was a considerable risk, as Japanese officials regularly inspected the POW camps. After internally debating on multiple scenarios to fool Japanese officials, Adun and other resistance leaders came up with a risky scheme; report that McGarry died in captivity and smuggle his "lifeless" body out of the camp via a makeshift coffin.[22] On April 14, 1945, Adundetcharat assigned a Thai policeman to remove McGarry from his cell. Should the Japanese catch up with the policeman's lies, Arun would disclaim that the order was forged and declare that he would take swift actions against the crime, further preserving his reputation with the Japanese while secretly working undercover for the Thai resistance movement. McGarry was taken to the Customs Department boat docked on the Chao Phraya river behind the OSS safehouse. To reduce the possibility of an encounter with Japanese soldiers, Seri Thai agents steered the boat through a network of canals that would eventually lead to the Gulf of Siam. When Japanese patrol boats were in close proximity, a Seri Thai officer

---

[21] Nicol Smith and Blake Clark, *Into Siam, Underground Kingdom*, (Indianapolis: The Bobbs-Merrill Company, 1946), 20.
[22] Ibid.

would hop on deck and begin a 'ramvong' (รำวง), a Thai style folk-dance incorporating simple hand movements and footwork accompanied by music played using traditional Thai instruments. The enthusiastic dancing and singing served as a distraction as well as a cover to drown our cries from other POWs who were traveling with McGarry, some of which suffered from PTSD and delirium.[23] After entering the Gulf of Siam, the boat headed south to the province of Prachuab Kiri Khan, where it remained hidden until the arrival of the OSS PBY Catalina. After boarding the Catalina, McGarry arriving in Ceylon (present-day Sri Lanka) and was then transferred to a B-24 bomber aircraft which made its way towards Kunming, China. Waiting for him on the runway was Chennault and two of his AVG comrades, reunited after three years.[24]

U.S. vs Britain, OSS vs SOE, and everything in between

As mentioned previously in the previous chapter, tensions were rising between the United States' OSS and the British SOE. The reasons for the ongoing tensions were fourfold. First, it was undeniable that the competitiveness between the two intelligence groups was rooted in

---

[23] Bergin, "OSS and Free Thai Operations in World War II," 18.
[24] Bob Bergin interview with AVG and Fourteenth Air Force pilot Edward Rector and Charles Older. As written in Bergin, "OSS and Free Thai Operations in World War II," 18.

the respective country's political stance and post-war prospects for Thailand. Thailand's declaration of war against the British carried lingering resentment. Despite Britain's partnership with the Seri Thai movement, officials in London were fixated on having Thailand pay the price for their involvement with Japan as well as surrender concessions on the Malay Peninsula.[25] The U.S. was concerned with this mentality, as they believed that if the SOE managed to establish contact inside Thailand before the OSS, they could potentially "freeze OSS out of Thai operations", successfully taking the lead in Thai intelligence operations and defining the post-war reality for not only Thailand but the rest of Southeast Asia.[26]

The second reason was in terms of the gap in efficiency and effectiveness between the intelligence group and their Free Thai counterpart. Compared to the OSS and their resistance fighters, the SOE and their Free Thai coalition was a small group that lacked proper resources to train and arm their Thai agents. As such, compared to the OSS that continuously launched successful infiltration missions, the SOE's actions were limited to radio communication and parachuting.

On a third note, Thai resistance fighters from Britain were part of the Pioneer Corps, military labor unit reserved for enemy aliens.[27] This continued categorization of Thais as criminals despite their willingness to sacrifice their lives for the Thai-British coalition, stained the or-

---

[25] Ibid., 100.
[26] Bergin, "OSS and Free Thai Operations in World War II," 13.
[27] Reynolds, *Thailand's Secret War*, 26.

ganization with underlying tension, overall impacting the effectiveness of the coalition as a whole.

The fourth and final note was the differing size in the network. Unlike SOE, the OSS gained a helpful domestic political partner in the Department of State, which supported OSS activities regarding Thailand. Because there was practically no U.S. interest in Thailand at the time, the Department of State had little competition from other U.S. agencies and more freedom in creating a consistent U.S. policy toward Bangkok than the UK had. Although the Free Thai never engaged in a large scale uprising against the Japanese, the OSS had guerrilla-training programs in place and clandestine radio stations relaying intelligence back to the Allies. In effect, the OSS had placed itself in a position to undermine the Japanese occupation of Thailand.

Everything changed on the morning of August 9, 1945. While OSS officers Alec MacDonald and Jim Thompson were en route to prepare for a parachute mission to infiltrate "214 Americans and 56 Free Thai to train 12 guerrilla battalions of 500 men each.", a pilot who entered the C-47 cabin shouting "It's over... the goddamn war is over!".[28] The sounds of confusion, shouting, and sobbing were eventually overtaken by a growing cry of celebration: "Chai Yo!". Despite having at least 50,000 armed resistance fighters ready to launch an attack, the war in Thailand concluded with Japanese formal surrender on September 2, 1945. Pridi and Prime

---

[28] Alec MacDonald, *A Wandering Spy Was I* (Kearney: Morris Publishing, 1997), 26.

Minister Khuang moved quickly, annulling the 1942 declaration of war. Alas, the Thai resistance movement evolved amid unusual international politics and ended under unusual international politics. By the end of the war, the Free Thai became one of the largest resistance movements in the sheer size of its membership which represented all members and elements of Thai society.

Chapter Five

Tragedy, Global Superpowers, the United Nations, and Other Post-War Aftermaths

The United States continues to regard Thailand as an independent state. We do not recognize the present Thai government. We continue to recognize as "Minister of Thailand" the Thai Minister in Washington, who has denounced his government's cooperation with Japan. We regard with sympathy a free Thai movement in which the Thai Minister in Washington is a prominent figure. We have not made and we do not contemplate making at this time any political commitment to any particular Thai national or Thai group prejudicing the future political situation. We favor restoration to Thailand of complete freedom as a sovereign state and we favor creation in Thailand of a government which will represent the free will of the Thai people.

—The Department of State to the British Embassy, March 20, 1944. Document handed by Assistant Secretary of State Adolf A. Berle to British Ambassador to the United States Edward Wood, 1st Earl of Halifax.[1]

The Tragedy in the Grand Palace

King Ananda returned to Thailand with his family after the conclusion of the war. Despite his unfamiliarity with kingship due to his young age, King Ananda quickly won the hearts of Thai people longing for a king since

---

[1] U.S. Department of State, *Foreign Relations of the United States: Diplomatic Papers*, 1944, The Near East, South Asia, and Africa, The Far East, Volume V, Document 1245.

the onslaught of the war. One of his most memorable acts included defusing the social, post-war tensions between ethnic Chinese and Thais in Sampheng Lane in Bangkok's Chinatown. Unfortunately, tragedy struck on June 9, 1946, when King Ananda was found deceased in his bedchambers.

Recognizing the mounting pressure from the Thai public and international news outlets, government officials ordered a special commission of inquiry to investigate the King's mysterious death. The investigation unit comprised of fifteen medical experts, one of which was American doctor Edwin C. Cort.[2] Cort had been a close friend of Prince Mahidol, the King's father. When Prince Mahidol was unable to enroll in medical residency after graduating from Harvard Medical School due to his royal status, the Prince chose to work at McCormick Hospital in Chiang Mai. With mutual interests in studies around malaria and tuberculosis, the Prince met and befriended American missionary and hospital director, Dr. Edwin C. Cort.[3] The request for Cort, an American foreigner, to examine the cause of death of his friend's son's highlights the growing trust and bond between Thailand and the United States post-World War II.

---

[2] Gilbert King, "Long Live the King." Smithsonian.com, Smithsonian Institution, September 28, 2011, www.smithsonianmag.com/history/long-live-the-king-1-91081660/. (accessed March 18, 2019).

[3] U.S. State Department Libraries – Consulate General of the United States of America, Chiang Mai, Thailand, *Two Nations One Friendship 180 Years*, May 2013.

Queen Mother Sangwal (center) with her sons King Ananda Mahidol (left) and Prince Bhumibol Adulyadej (right).
Source: Wikimedia Commons

After a detailed autopsy as well as several X-ray examinations, medical officers concluded that there was a higher probability that the King's death was a result of an assassination rather than suicide. Despite the conclusion, rumors began to circulate, with initial press noting it was an accidental death, reasoning that the King's peculiar fascination with firearms might have caused the gun to go off by mistake.[4] Others were more skeptical, claiming that it was the work of Japanese agents in an act of vengeance.[5] Pridi, recognizing the rising social unrest both from civilians and journalists, declared a state of national emergency. Soon after, King Ananda's brother and newly crowned King Bhumibol moved back to Switzerland with his mother to finish his studies. The move was to prepare him for his new role as monarch as well to avoid entangling himself with the current political climate, which by now, was spiraling out of control due to the clashes between the military regime and the civilian government.

The King returned four years later in 1950, this time, surrounding himself with Western-educated diplomats and advisors to tackle the complexities of preserving the monarchy within the confines of a military-ruled political structure. The U.S. and Thailand continued to build strong relations. The United States Central Intelligence (a successor of the OSS as of 1947) assisted the country in establishing the Thai Border Patrol Police (ตำรวจตระเวนชายแดนสำนักงานตำรวจแห่งชาติ). In an equally significant event, the U.S. also fostered an anti-community ally in Thailand to combat Vietnam. By 1954, the U.S. formed the Southeast Asia Treaty Organi-

---

[4] Associated Press, "Gun Kills Siam's Young King; Palace Death Held Accident," *New York Times,* June 10, 1946, https://www.nytimes.com/1946/06/10/archives/gun-kills-siams-young-king-palace-death-held-accident-found-dead.html. (accessed April 2, 2019).

[5] William Stevenson and Richard Rodgers, *The Revolutionary King: The True-Life sequel to The King and I.* (London: Constable & Company Limited, 1999), 55.

zation (SEATO), granting the U.S. a "multilateral defense pact in conformity with the U.N. Charter" and in turn, protected Thailand from Chinese communist advancement coming from the north.[6] Earning the full support of King Bhumipol earning, the U.S. was granted permission to establish military bases in Udon Thani, Korat, and U-Tapao during the Vietnam war era. With the rise of King Bhumipol's popularity, the increase in anti-communist countermeasures, and the closure of the late King's case by the Royal forces, his Majesty King Ananda's mysterious death became a distant memory.

As mentioned in previous chapters, though the U.S. and Great Britain were both supported by the Free Thai movement's activities throughout the war, they possessed staunch politico-ideological differences in post-war negotiation for Thailand.

The American Model

With a record of over 150 years of friendship, it is undeniably difficult to summarize the U.S. and Thai relationships within a subsection of a chapter. Missionary activities and the role of American advisors in Thailand's political negotiations were some of the first instances of fostering goodwill between the two countries. The 1833 *Siamese-American Treaty of Amity and Commerce* played a significant role in the modernization of the Thai

---

[6] Wiwat Mungkandi, "Thai-American Relations in Historical Perspective," *United States-Thailand Relations*, (1985): 5.

economy and missionaries helped bring the English language to the forefront of Thai education. Out of admiration for the American missionaries' knowledge in educational and medical fields, under Thai custom, they were soon referred to as "doctor" (หมอ), a nickname given to those who have garnered great respect from Thais.

Further relationships that were built between the two countries were the interactions between the heads of state. King Mongkut established close relationships with U.S. presidents Franklin Pierce and James Buchanan. The most famous interaction was a February 14, 1861 letter the King wrote to Buchanan to offer a pair of elephants to be used in the American transportation system.[7] The letter, however, arrived when Lincoln had already succeeded Buchanan. Dealing with the implications of the Civil War at the time, Lincoln respectfully declined the gesture and noted the U.S.'s growing dependence on steam for internal commerce. He did, however, take the King's gift of a sword with a gold and silver scabbard and placed it among the U.S. archives of gifts from foreign heads of state.[8] His Majesty Bhumibol Adulyadej later mentioned this event before the two Houses of the U.S. Congress on June 29, 1960 stating, "No other objective than to provide a friend with what he lacked, in the same spirit in which the American aid program is likewise offered".[9]

---

[7] Pichair Vasnason, "Thai-U.S. Cultural Relations," *United States-Thailand Relations*, (1986): 39-49.
[8] Ibid., 39.
[9] Senate Resolution 9 (1960). 115th Congress 1st Session.

June 29, 1960, Washington, DC, USA—His Majesty Bhumibol Adulyadej Addresses the U.S. Congress. Seated behind him are Vice President Richard Nixon and Speaker of the House Sam Rayburn.
Source: Wikimedia Commons

U.S. post-war policy with Thailand was one that considered Thailand as an enemy-occupied territory rather than that of a Japanese ally. The U.S. confirmed it's unconditional support for the country and the Free Thai movement, stating, "We favor restoration to Thailand of complete freedom as a sovereign state and we favor creation in Thailand of a government which will represent the free will of the Thai people".[10] This statement would go down as being one of the strongest affirmations of U.S. support for Thai sovereignty. With a history of strong ties and friendships, it would be no surprise that the U.S. came to the defense of Thailand during post-war negotiations.

The British Model

While the British recognized that the Seri Thai movement was a powerful resistance movement that allowed them to collect and compile intelligence on Japanese activities, they dulled out substantial punishments and harsh post-war policy decisions. One of these decisions included the Thai occupation of British colonial territories, which was a topic of constant contention via diplomatic exchanges between the British Foreign Office and the U.S. State Department. Britain wished to regain the colonial holdings they lost during 1943, which territories included Kedah, Perlis, Kelantan, and Terengganu in Malaya, and parts of the Shan State in Burma (otherwise known as Saharat Thai Doem). Aiming to restore their dominant pre-war role in Thailand's trade they also called for financial restitution for losses that were sustained by their firms, particularly in resource-rich Ma-

---

[10] U.S. Department of State, *Foreign Relations, 1944, Volume V*, Washington D.C.: Government Printing Office, 1945, 1316-1317.

laya.[11] Only when British demands were met, would Thailand be allowed membership into the United Nations. The French even engaged in efforts to block Thailand's admission into the United Nations and only ceding when Indochinese territories[12] were returned. The reality was, Britain and France's refusal to acknowledge Thai sovereignty was not rooted in their disapproval of the country's political structure or the invalidation of the Free Thai movement, but rather of their own personal insecurities in losing their colonial lands. These territories would later dissolve into their respective states who were now pushing back against imperial rule.[13]

There was no doubt that Britain's refusal to recognize guarantee a Free Thailand was also rooted in Britain's feelings of betrayal in Thailand's declaration of war against the country in January 1942. This was clearly reflected in a 1944 statement by British Minister, George Bailey Sansom:

A country with a long traditional friendship with us has, though admittedly under pressure from Japan,

---

[11] Reynolds, *Thailand's Secret War*, 369-372.

[12] These territories are today's Luang Prabang Range in Laos and Battambang, Banteay Meanchey, Oddar Meanchey, Siem Reap and parts of Preah Vihear Province in Cambodia.

[13] Southeast Asian Countries that gained Independence from British rule included Myanmar (Burma) in 1948, Brunei in 1984, Malaysia in 1968, and Singapore (who was previously under British rule prior to and during WWII and then gained independence from Malaysia in 1965). Southeast Asian Countries that gained independence from French rule included Vietnam in 1945, Laos in 1949, and Cambodia in 1953. Thailand previously held concessions in Burma, Cambodia, and Laos.

> *betrayed that friendship. Not content with collaborating with our enemy and despite her treaty of non-aggression with us the quisling government of Luang Pibul took the initiative in declaring war upon us. For these acts Thailand is already paying the price and will undoubtedly pay a yet heavier price as the war reaches her territories. It is still possible for the people of Thailand to do something to save themselves from the worst consequences of their betrayal, and they will be judged by the efforts that they make to redeem themselves from the position in which the action of their present régime has placed them. Like other countries in like case "They must work their passage home". If they do so they can look to this country to support the emergence of a free and independent Thailand after the war is over.*[14]

One cannot help but pick out Britain's hypocrisy in the matter when comparing the attitude they had towards their European neighbors. Specifically, when Italy surrendered to Allied forces in October 1943 and switched sides a month later, Britain immediately took initiatives to back traditional, conservative Italian elites to help maintain political, societal, and economic order in the country.[15] On the contrary, Britain's recommendation

---

[14] Document handed from British Minister George Bailey Sansom to the Deputy Director of the Office of Far Eastern Affairs Dr. Joseph W. Ballantine, February 26, 1944.

[15] Niall MacGalloway, "All the King's Men? British Official Policy Towards the Italian Resistance," *Retrospectives: A Postgraduate History Journal* 2, No. 1 (2013): 42-56.

for Thailand was to retire the country's old system of advisers and exchange it for advisers under one of the United Nations member countries as a form of a 'quasi-tutelary authority'.[16] The discrepancy between the policy of British policy towards Thailand and their policy towards European countries was further highlighted by the 1947 Paris Peace Treaty, an event in which Thailand was neither invited or included as associated power. While the British criticized Thailand's betrayal of friendship and lack of initiatives of their group's interaction with the Free Thai movement, they possessed "great hopes in resistance groups aiding them in liberating the [European] continent".[17] This point is furthered by London's continued attempts to seek out settlements based on measures of revenge and the facilitation of establishing a British presence in Southeast Asia.

One of the drivers behind the harsh British policy towards Thailand was due to the now-retired Sir Josiah Crosby. In an article that he published in October 1943, Crosby suggested the United Nations diminish the role of Thailand's military power, framing it as a part of a postwar settlement and opportunity for democracy to flourish in the nation. In another article he published a year later, Crosby argued that the country was "liable to punishment" and that there needed to be "some form of

---

[16] Nicholas Tarling, "Atonement Before Absolution: British Policy Towards Thailand During World War II," *Journal of the Siam Society* 66 (1978): 22-65.
[17] Ibid.

tutelage" after the end of the war, with one example offered to be the desolation of the Royal Thai Military.

While not all of Crosby's recommendations were presented to Thai officials for consideration, it is important to note that this undertone of 'atonement before and retribution' in exchange for access to the global playing field defined Anglo-Thai foreign policy for years to come.

Representatives attending the Singapore Conference. From left to right: Sir Robert Brooke-Popham (Commander-in-Chief, Far East); Mr. Alfred Duff Cooper (England); Sir Earle Page (Australia); Sir Archibald Clarke-Kerr (British Ambassador, Chungking); Sir Shenton Thomas (Governor of Malaya); Sir Geoffrey Layton (Commander-in-Chief, China Station). Sir Josiah Crosby (British Minister to Thailand) was not able to attend.
Source: National Portrait Gallery

The U.S. Foreign Policy Dominance

The U.S. postwar policy for Thailand prevailed. In 1946, Thailand accepted the U.S.'s compromise to cede territories acquired during the war in exchange for admission to the United Nations, wartime claims, and U.S. economic aid. The predominance of U.S. foreign policy over the British can be attributed to multiple fronts. First is the U.S.'s growing global influence. One cannot deny that comparatively, the U.S. emerged from the war economically, militarily, and politically stronger than when it first joined. Thus, the United State now held a new role as a major superpower that was able to shape peace negotiations according to their own terms.

In the framework of Thailand, the U.S. played a substantial role in refuting and redefining British post-war demands. Since the early stages of the war, the U.S. worked to protect Thailand's sovereignty from the British. In one instance, the OSS Detachment 404 research and analysis team concluded that the British were intentionally perpetuating the state of war within Thailand to use as a form of leverage in postwar demands.[18] This included welcoming an internal clash between Thailand and Japan, hoping that it would cause "a disastrous dissipation of Thai forces and chaotic political conditions," that would grant the British the opportunity for a military intervention disguised in the form of "liberation".[19] In another

---

[18] Reynolds, *Thailand's Secret War*, 371.
[19] "British Strategic Intentions in Southeast Asia II," August 2, 1945, *Reel 14*, M1642, USNA.

instance, as a result of Thailand's unique duality, the country managed to accumulate a substantial amount of grain surplus due to lack of agricultural damage as compared to their other Allied (or even Axis) counterparts. The British sought to capitalize on the opportunity and demand this surplus as war reparations.[20] Concerned about these intentions, the State Department increased efforts to supply the residence and backed the activists throughout their intelligence campaign. The OSS presence in Thailand and its successful partnership with the Seri Thai had opened the door for future U.S. foreign policy in Southeast Asia.

The U.S. also took steps to protect Thailand from British retribution and aggrandizement. In various distances, the U.S. spoke on Thailand's unique position as one of the few Asian nations actively favorable to capitalist democracy and that the current political leaders were open to establishing new intelligence forces to support the West in future wartime activities. Furthermore, Wiwar Mungkandi credits the strength of U.S. Thai relations defining the post-war narrative for Thailand, stating:

> "The "Seri-Thai' activities, the U.S. intervention in the British post-war demands on the Thais, and the U.S. support for Thai admission to the United Nations—all of these served as the first turning point in Thai-U.S. relations, which paved the way for a

---

[20] Nicholas Tarling, "An Attempt to Fly in the Face of the Ordinary Laws of Supply and Demand: The British and Siamese Rice, 1945–7," *Journal of the Siam Society* 75 (1987): 140-86.

"close and intense" cooperation in the post-1945 period".[21]

In an even more specific example, on February 9, 1945, the U.S. military authorities partnered with the State Department to adopt a paper written by the State-War-Navy Coordinating Committee (SWNCC). The paper argues that British suggestion of special controls over Thailand was "without merit" and that there should be no Allied control organs established in Thailand "beyond the immediate defeat of the common enemy."[22] This approach to Thailand post-war policy was later endorsed by the Joint Chiefs of Staff on June 27, 1945. The U.S.'s arguments on successes of the Seri-Thai and Britain's lack of justification for their post-war policies towards Thailand made it virtually impractical for the British to seek political control in Thailand.

The second reason for the success of U.S. policy towards Thailand was the decline of British Imperialism. Colonialism was becoming less economically and politically viable for the British. The country was slowly emerging from post-war austerity and had accumulated around $4.33bn (£2.2bn) worth in war-debt.[23] While

---

[21] Wiwat Mungkandi. "Thai-American Relations in Historical Perspective," 3-23.
[22] SWNCC5/2 and JCS1271/3, ABC092, US-Thailand, 1945, RG165, USNA.
[23] The United Kingdom made its 50th and last payment to the U.S. in the closing Friday 2006 in the amount of $83.25m (£42.5m). The United Kingdom's total debt paid back to the U.S.'s lend lease program was

Chapter 5: Tragedy, Global Superpowers, the United Nations...

Britain's new government, led by the Labour Party Prime Minister Clement Attlee, initially sought to increase production and exports from the colonies, he soon resigned to the fact when confronted with pushback and growing nationalistic sentiment from those very same colonies. Financing efforts to attempt to halt or stabilize uprisings through military and political intervention soon became an expensive liability and set the tone for the eventual decline of British imperialism.[24] No other case study comes close to exemplifying this shift than with the case of Indian Independence in 1947.

Various events foreshadowed the country's yearning for full independence from the British, with some including the Indian Rebellion of 1857, the Jallianwala Bagh massacre, Bengal famine, and Gandhi and the Indian National Congress's 'Quit India' movement. Fighting for self-governance, frustrated by heavy loss of Indian lives fighting for Britain's battles[25], and disappointed with Britain's failure to uphold their promise in granting the country independence in return for the country's wartime contributions set off a nationwide call-to-arms. The crown soon realized that 200 years of

---

nearly double that which was loaned in 1945 and 1946. Source: *BBC News, UK settles WWII debts to allies* (December 29, 2006).

[24] Ian Kikuchi, "The End of the British Empire After the Second World War," iwm.org.uk, Imperial War Museum, February 6, 2018, https://www.iwm.org.uk/history/the-end-of-the-british-empire-after-the-second-world-war. (accessed May 1, 2019).

[25] By the end of the war, the British Indian Army was the largest volunteer army in the world with over 2 million men. That was more than the combined troops of Australia, New Zealand, Canada, and South Africa.

imperialism were no match against an armed rebellion back by the support of over 320 million people.²⁶ This defeat set off a domino effect in other colonies and soon other nationalist movements challenged British rule. Ian Kikuchi further validates this point, stating:

> *"In 1947 India, having contributed enormously to Britain's war effort, became independent. Less than a year later, communist guerrillas launched a violent campaign aimed at forcing Britain from Malaya. Thousands were killed, but an effective political and military response prevented a Communist take-over. Malaya became an independent democracy on 31 August 1957. In the Middle East, Britain hurriedly abandoned Palestine in 1948. Ghana became Britain's first African colony to reach independence in 1957. By 1967 more than 20 British territories were independent."*

Viceroy Lord Curzon foreshadowed the independence of India as the cause for the end of Britain's imperial rule, stating in 1902, "As long as we rule India we are the greatest power in the world. If we lose it we shall drop straightway to a third-rate power".²⁷ Already hurt by lingering debt, the British defeat in India and impeding revolutions disrupted the Empire's financial and eco-

---

²⁶ Shashi Tharoor, *An Era of Darkness: The British Empire in India*. (New Delhi: Aleph Book Company, 2016), 100.

²⁷ Tristram Hunt, Cities of Empire: *The British Colonies and the Creation of the Urban World* (Basingstoke: Macmillan, 2014), 357.

Chapter 5: TRAGEDY, GLOBAL SUPERPOWERS, THE UNITED NATIONS...

nomic independence, essentially the foundation of the entire imperial system.

Britain often found themselves tangled in the affairs of other nationalist movements across the world. In 1945, the country attempted to aid the Dutch to secure Indonesia but was met with immediate retaliation from revolutionary forces in Surabaya, the second-largest city in the country. The Battle of Surabaya became one of the bloodiest battles during the Indonesian National Revolution and became a symbol of Indonesia resistance, with November 10, 1945, is celebrated annually as Hero's Day (Hari Pahlawan).[28] Shortly after Britain's loss in Indonesia, the country disbanded the largely forgotten SEAC (Anglo-American South East Asia Command), an organization that Americans noted was less about building bridges in Southeast Asia and more about "Sav[ing] England's Asiatic Colonies".[29] An animated movie directed by Aryanto Yuniawan was released in 2015 and centers on Indonesia's role in World War II and the revolution that was ignited shortly after. Since its release, it has galvanized international awards and recognition.

Other British entanglements with nationalist movements incidents further highlighted the U.S.'s growing anti-colonial attitude, those of which included the U.S. denunciation of imperialism during the 1949 Liyan riots in Tripoli, the fall of Burma in 1948, and Suez Canal Crisis in Panama. Regarding the latter, the U.S. had sup-

---

[28] Merle Calvin Ricklefs, *A History of Modern Indonesia: c. 1300 to the Present.* (Basingstoke: Macmillan, 1981), 217.
[29] Bergin, "OSS and Free Thai Operations in World War II," 21.

ported the withdrawal of British troops from the country since the 1946 agreement. In 1952, Egyptians called for the right to self-determination, leading to a 1954 decision to pressure the end of the British presence in the Canal Zone. Frustrated with British impasse on military withdrawal and the U.S. failing to keep their promise in funding the construction of the Aswan Dam, Egyptian President Nassar nationalization the canal in 1956, leading up to an event that was coined the Suez Canal Crisis. The U.S., disappointed with the British for undergoing secret military consultations without informing the U.S., threatened all three nations with economic sanctions.[30] In response, British, French, and Israeli troops withdrew from the Canal Zone in 1956. Britain failed to evolve its foreign policy to meet the needs of countries and communities that were fighting for self-determination. The U.S. used this reluctance to their advantage, arguing that the British refused to have a happy, prosperous, independent native state in South East Asia" and instead, suggested to the Thais that they would take up their role as protector from the British.[31] Rather than transition their role as mediators and middle powers, the British continued to cling onto the prospects of their broken ideology, evidently leading to the downfall of the Empire years later. An empire that once possessed lands from

---

[30] Office of the Historian "The Suez Crisis, 1956," history.state.gov, Office of the Historian MILESTONES: 1953–1960, https://history.state.gov/milestones/1953-1960/suez. (accessed July 25, 2019).

[31] Intelligence Proposal, n.d., Folder 3, Box 319, Entry 210, RG 226, USNA.

the Caribbean to Asia, was now reduced to a supporting role in comparison with the leader of the free world, the United States.

Epilogue

Viewing Thailand's decision from another perspective, one could argue that the country made its decision to follow the American model even before the conclusion of the war. As the U.S.'s global position gradually grew throughout the war, so did Thailand's shift to the side with American allies. Growing the resistance movement was Thailand's strategy in gaining American support, allowing them to simultaneously avoiding British imposition of both economic and political restitutions.

Although disturbed by the continued British unwillingness to address him officially and Jacques' report that Mountbatten would have full power to negotiate political as well as military matters, Pridi carried out the first set of "suggestions." He issued a statement denouncing the declaration of war and treaties with Japan at the National Assembly on 16 August, despite Jacques' concern that doing so immediately might provoke the Japanese. Pridi advised SEAC by radio of his willingness to send representatives to Kandy, but asked to be informed of the subjects to be discussed "so that they may take with the appropriate authority."

A quote that perfectly summarizes Thailand's strategy throughout the war is one that Robert W. Lawson, a counterintelligence (X-2) OSS officer, stated in his final report:

> During the war the Siamese Government played a two-sided game with extreme skill. If the Japanese had won the war, the Siamese Government would have been in a strong position with the Japanese Government and would have been able to prove the great assistance which that government had given Japan. With the Allies winning the war, the Siamese Government was still in a position to point out to the Allies all the assistance and information which they had given the Allies, even though legally there were the allies of an enemy nation. The Siamese Government has been so successful in this diplomatic maneuver that today it is difficult to know where the true sympathy of the Siamese lay. They are now undoubtedly wholeheartedly for the Allies since they are the victors.[1]

Lawson warned that the Thai seemed to be continuing this "two-faced policy," noting that Thai carefully kept American and British forces separated during social festivities while simultaneously spreading damaging rumors, instigating incidents of preferential treatment, and ultimately, engaging in tactics that drove a wedge be-

---

[1] Robert W. Lawson, "General Report of the Situation in Bangkok," October 9, 1945, *Folder 274, Box 24, Entry 110*, RG 226, USNA.

tween the two countries. Of the lavish hospitality the Allies had received, he added, "In several cases, our most ardent hosts on investigation turned out to have been equally ardent hosts to the Japanese during their stay in the country".[2]

While a majority of the book delves into Thailand's international strategy during wartime, this book aimed to reflect on the internal policies that were enacted and the repercussions that continue to follow it. As mentioned in the previous chapter, an issue that continues to impact Thailand to this day is its complicated, and oftentimes unbridled, relationship with the military. Since the end of absolute monarchy in 1932, the Thai military has undergone 19 military coups and was complicit in almost every reinstatement of the prime ministership.[3] After the ousting of democratically elected Yingluck Shinawatra in 2011, the country is yet again under military rule.[4] This poses several complications for Thailand moving forward.

On the economic front, other than the National Assembly, no other check and balance system exist for administering the country budget. This lack of proper government institutions or proper checks and balance system to counteract the military has allowed the military to

---

[2] Ibid.

[3] Freedom House, "Freedom in the World 2015: The Annual Survey of Political Rights and Civil Liberties," *Freedom House*, (2015): 678.

[4] As of publishing this book, General Prayuth Chan-ocha, a retired Royal Thai Army General Officer, currently serves as the country's Prime Minister. He is the country's 29th Prime Minister.

have full jurisdiction over both the finances of both the military and the entire country.

On the societal front, Phibun's centralization policies led to the curse of military favoritism. In fact, the National Council for Peace and Order (the country's military junta coalition) nominated 200 members solely from three categories "the military, the bureaucrats, and the PDRC supporters". With the military holding majority within parliament, areas such as civil society, elections, and transparent budgeting have been held back overall restricting the country's democratic transition. Unfortunately, rather than recognizing that their actions run the risk of stymieing democratic progression, the Thai military views, and continued to view itself as the vanguard of national unity and the savior of the nation in times of distress.

Furthermore, the country continues to deal with subnational political issues, specifically ethnic fractionalization and political unrest in the country's Deep South. On top of Phibun's 'Thaification' policies, he also enacted laws and regulations that centralize political, societal, and economic control in Bangkok. This had and continues to have, extremely negative effects on Thailand's ethnic Malay Muslim population, perpetuating political marginalization, and systematic discrimination against Malay Muslims and exacerbating ethnic conflict in the provinces of Narathiwat, Yala, and Pattani (which house a large percentage of ethnic Malay Muslims). Examples of laws enacted by the Phibun government included stipping the ability of the three provinces to elect their own governments and representatives[5], strengthening the role of 'state-appointed' governors[6], taking full control of provincial budgets and delivery of local services[7], and canceling development initiatives and state investments, leading to inadequate health services and lack of academic resources.[8] The legacy of the Phibun government's centralized crackdown and prioritizations of policies that benefit the wellbeing of ethnic, Buddhist Thais over their Muslim minority, have caused the latter to feel isolated, disrespected, and marginalized leading incidents of armed conflict and violence that government officials continue to struggle with today. If Thailand wishes to solve its ethnic tensions, not only does it have to look to restructure this hierarchical, top-down subnational framework, but it has to allow for Muslim voices to be heard.

Finally, whether you as a reader are studying and analyzing Thailand through the lens of an eager reader who loves history, a student who is just trying to get sources for their finals paper, or an academic scholar eager to write a two page review critiquing my entire thesis, I hope that we can all agree that Thailand's ability to navigate through a highly complicated and crowded political arena with dip-

---

[5] Duncan McCargo, *Tearing apart the land: Islam and legitimacy in Southern Thailand* (Cornell University Press, 2008), 70-75.
[6] Ibid.
[7] Adam Burke, Pauline Tweedie, and Ora-Orn Poocharoen. "The Contested Corners of Asia: The Case of Southern Thailand," *The Asia Foundation*, (2013): 67
[8] Akiko Horiba, "Overview and Context of Thailand's Deep South Conflict." *Asia Peacebuilding Initiatives*. N.p., (2013).

lomatic exchanges, negotiations, and let's face it, pure trickery, made it one of the biggest victors of World War II. The country was well aware of the growing predominance of U.S. policy and the decline of the British model and utilized the situation to their advantage; another reflection on how Thailand utilizes the concept of duality. Using the polarization of both nations is nothing new to Thailand, as we have shown in previous chapters. Thailand's fight for independence through strategies of selective disengagement, territorial compromise, and political duality, all for the sake of protecting the nation and its people, was its method for preserving sovereignty. Whether it was through Phibun's bidding for improved international treaties or Pridi's partnership with the U.S. and Great Britain, no other country in the world came out of the war through pure political maneuvering intact as did Thailand. That in itself, speaks to the unbreakable goal of Siamese sovereignty.

Bibliography

Books

Aaron Asadi, Ross Andrews, and Dave Harfield, *All About History – Book of Kings & Queens* (Imagine Publishing Ltd., 2014).

Alec MacDonald, *A Wandering Spy Was I* (Kearney: Morris Publishing, 1997).

Anne Booth, *Colonial Legacies: Economic and Social Development in East and Southeast Asia* (University of Hawaii Press 2007).

Barend Jan Terwiel, *A History of Modern Thailand, 1767-1942* (St. Lucia: University of Queensland Press, 1983).

Bōeichō Bōei Kenshujo Senshishitsu, *Daibon' ei rikugunbu (The Army Section of Imperial General Head-quarters)*, (Tokyo, 1968-1974).

Chris Baker and Pasuk Phongpaichit, *A History of Ayuttaya: Siam in the Early Modern World* (Cambridge: Cambridge University Press, 2017).

Chris Baker and Pasuk Phongpaichit, *A History of Thailand* (Cambridge: Cambridge University Press, 2014).

David K. Wyatt, *Thailand: A Short History* (New Haven: Yale University Press, 2003).

Duncan McCargo, *Tearing apart the land: Islam and legitimacy in Southern Thailand* (Cornell University Press, 2008).

E. Bruce Reynolds, *Thailand and Japan's Southern Advance 1940--1945* (New York: St. Martin's Press, 1994).

E. Bruce Reynolds, *Thailand's Secret War: OSS, SOE and the Free Thai Underground During World War II* (Cambridge: Cambridge University Press, 2010)

John B. Haseman, *The Thai Resistance Movement During World War II* (Chiang Mai: Silkworm Books, 2002).

Kobkua Suwannathat-Pian, *Thailand's Durable Premier: Phibun through Three Decades, 1932–1957* (Kuala Lumpur: Oxford University Press, 1995).

Likhit Dhiravegin, *Siam and Colonialism, 1855-1909: An Analysis of Diplomatic Relations* (Bangkok: Thai Watana Panich, 1974).

Manich Jumsai, *History of Anglo-Thai Relations* (Bangkok: Chalermnit Press, 1970).

Malai Chumpanit (มาลัย ชูพินิจ) (pseudonym Chanthana 'นายฉันทนา') X.O. Group เรื่องภายในขบวนเสรีไทย, (Thai Panit Publications, 1964).

Naoko Simazu, *Japan, Race and Equality: The Racial Equality Proposal of 1919* (Routledge, 2002).

Nidhi Eoseewong (นิธิ เอี่ยวศรีวงศ์), *Karn Muang Thai Samai Phra Chao Krung Thonburi (การเมืองไทยสมัยพระเจ้ากรุงธนบุรี)*, (Tichon Publishing, 1993).

Prince Damrong Rajanubhab, *The Chronicle of Our War with the Burmese* (Chonburi: White Lotus Co Ltd., 2001).

Rod Beattie, *The Death Railway: A Brief History of the Thailand-Burma Railway* (Image Makers Co., Ltd, 2005).

Richard James Aldrich, *The Key to the South: Britain, the United States, and Thailand During the Approach of the Pacific War, 1929-1942* (Oxford: Oxford University Press, 1993).

Thamsook Numnonda, *Thailand and the Japanese Presence, 1941-45.* (Singapore: ISEAS Publishing, 1977).

Thawi Bunyaket, *Thailand and World War II (ไทยกับสงครามโลกครั้งที่ 2)* (Bangkok: Sripanya Press, 1966).

U.S. Department of the Army, *Thailand Operations Record, Japanese Monograph #177* (Tokyo: Headquarters Army Forces Far East, 1953).

Wanthani, ed., *Neung Satawan Suphasawat*, (Bangkok, 2000).

William Stevenson and Richard Rodgers, *The Revolutionary King: The True-Life sequel to The King and I*. (London: Constable & Company Limited, 1999).

Zachary Shore, *Blunder: Why Smart People Make Bad Decisions* (Bloomsbury Publishing USA, 2010).

Journals/ Academic Articles

Adam Burke, Pauline Tweedie, and Ora-Orn Poocharoen. "The Contested Corners of Asia: The Case of Southern Thailand," *The Asia Foundation, (2013).*

Akiko Horiba, "Overview and Context of Thailand's Deep South Conflict." *Asia Peacebuilding Initiatives.* N.p., (2013).

Bob Bergin, "OSS and Free Thai Operations in World War II," *Studies in Intelligence*, Vol. 55, No. 4 (2011).

E. Bruce Reynolds, "'International Orphans: The Chinese in Thailand during World War II'", *Journal of Southeast Asian Studies,* Vol. 28, No. 2 (1997).

E. Bruce Reynolds, "Phibun Songkhram and Thai Nationalism in the Fascist Era," *European Journal of East Asian Studies,* Volume 3, (2004).

Freedom House, "Freedom in the World 2015: The Annual Survey of Political Rights and Civil Liberties," *Freedom House*, (2015).

H.C. Quaritch-Wales, "Thailand-Key to the Coming Attack on Japan," *Asia and the Americas Volume 42,* (1942).

James V. Martin "Thai-American Relations in World War II," *The Journal of Asian Studies* Volume 22, No. 4, (1963).

Keith Hart, "A Note on the Military Participation of Siam in the First World War." *Journal of Siam Society 1981-1990* Vol. 69 (1981). Originally published in the *New York Times* in 1918.

Kobkua Suwannathat-Pian, "Thai Wartime Leadership Reconsidered: Phibun and Pridi Kobkua Suwannathat-Pian," *Journal of Southeast Asian Studies* Volume 27, Issue 1. (The Japanese Occupation in Southeast Asia)., (1996).

Margaret Landon, "Thailand Under the Japanese." *Asia and the Americas,* Issue 44.9 (1944).

Merle Calvin Ricklefs, *A History of Modern Indonesia: c. 1300 to the Present.* (Basingstoke: Macmillan, 1981).

Nai Samrej, "That Thailand May Be Free," *Asia and the Americas,* (February 1945).

Niall MacGalloway, "All the King's Men? British Official Policy Towards the Italian Resistance," *Retrospectives: A Postgraduate History Journal* 2, No. 1 (2013).

Nicholas Tarling, "An Attempt to Fly in the Face of the Ordinary Laws of Supply and Demand: The British and Siamese Rice, 1945–7," *Journal of the Siam Society* 75 (1987).

Nicholas Tarling, "Atonement Before Absolution: British Policy Towards Thailand During World War II," *Journal of the Siam Society* 66 (1978).

Nicol Smith and Blake Clark, *Into Siam, Underground Kingdom,* (Indianapolis: The Bobbs-Merrill Company, 1946).

Nik Anuar Nik Mahmud, "British Policy and Thailand, *1939-1940,"* Jebat: Malaysian Journal of History, Politics and Strategic Studies*, Volume 9 (1979).

Pichair Vasnason, "Thai-U.S. Cultural Relations," *United States-Thailand Relations,* (1986)

Royal Thai Government Gazette, *Melody and Lyrics of the National Anthem,* Volume 56, 1939, 2643.

Shashi Tharoor, *An Era of Darkness: The British Empire in India.* (New Delhi: Aleph Book Company, 2016).

Sunit Chutintaranond, "The Image of the Burmese enemy in Thai Perceptions and Historical Writings," *Journal of the Siam Society* (1992).

Tristram Hunt, *Cities of Empire: The British Colonies and the Creation of the Urban World,* (Basingstoke: Macmillan, 2014).

Walter A. Ewing, "Opportunity and Exclusion: A Brief History of U.S. Immigration Policy," *Immigration Policy Center* (2012).

Walter Fitzmaurice, "Thailand, Ally in Secret, Snooped under Japs' Noses", *Newsweek*, 3. 9. 1945.

Wiwat Mungkandi. "Thai-American Relations in Historical Perspective" *United States-Thailand Relations*, (1986).

Online Articles

Associated Press, "Gun Kills Siam's Young King; Palace Death Held Accident," *New York Times,* June 10, 1946, https://www.nytimes.com/1946/06/10/archives/gun-kills-siams-young-king-palace-death-held-accident-found-dead.html. (accessed April 2, 2019).

Australian Government Department of Veteran Affairs, "Rŏmusha Recruitment," Anzac Centenary Program, https://anzacportal.dva.gov.au/history/conflicts/burma-thailand-railway-and-hellfire-pass/burma-thailand-railway-and-hellfire-2 (accessed Dec 18, 2018).

Australian Government Department of Veteran Affairs, "The Burma-Thailand Railway and Hellfire Pass," Anzac Centenary Program, https://anzacportal.dva.gov.au/history/conflicts/thaiburma-railway-and-hellfire-pass (accessed Dec 18, 2018).

BBC News, UK settles WWII debts to allies, December 29, 2006, http://news.bbc.co.uk/2/hi/uk/6215847.stm. (accessed January 2, 2019).

CIA World Factbook: https://www.cia.gov/library/publications/the-world-factbook/geos/th.html

Eleanor Albert, "ASEAN: The Association of Southeast Asian Nations", *Council on Foreign Relations*, https://www.cfr.org/backgrounder/asean-association-southeast-asian-nations (accessed September 23, 2019).

Gilbert King, "Long Live the King." Smithsonian.com, Smithsonian Institution, September 28, 2011, www.smithsonianmag.com/history/long-live-the-king-1-91081660/. (accessed March 18, 2019).

Ian Kikuchi, "The End of the British Empire After the Second World War," iwm.org.uk, Imperial War Museum, February 6, 2018, https://www.iwm.org.uk/history/the-end-of-the-british-empire-after-the-second-world-war. (accessed May 1, 2019).

Joe Leeds, "UPDATE: Introduction to the Legal System and Legal Research of the Kingdom of Thailand", *Hauser Global Law School Program*. NYU Law Global, November/December, 2016, https://www.nyulawglobal.org/globalex/Thailand1.html. (accessed August 1, 2019).

Office of the Historian "The Suez Crisis, 1956," history.state.gov, Office of the Historian MILESTONES: 1953–1960, https://history.state.gov/milestones/1953-1960/suez. (accessed July 25, 2019).

Professor Piset Noraniti Seetabut (ศาสตราจารย์พิเศษ นรนิติ เศรษฐบุตร) "(Chamkat Phalangkun) จำกัด พลางกูร," *King Prajadhipok Institute*, King Prajadhipok Institute, 2016. https://tinyurl.com/yynzb862. (accessed July 2, 2019).

U.S. Department of State, *Foreign Relations of the United States: Diplomatic Papers*, 1944, The Near East, South Asia, and Africa, The Far East, Volume V, Document 1245.

U.S. Department of State, *Foreign Relations, 1944, Volume V,* Washington D.C.: Government Printing Office, 1945, 1316-1317.

"World Population Prospects: The 2017 Revision". *esa.un.org*. United Nations Department of Economic and Social Affairs, Population Division.

Records/ Microfilm

Area Handbook for Thailand, CIA, (Washington, D.C., 1968).
"British Strategic Intentions in Southeast Asia II," August 2, 1945, *Reel 14, M1642*, USNA.
Crosby to FO, 3 August 1939, F10131.

Resources

Crosby to FO, July 5, 1940, F3690.

Document handed from British Minister George Bailey Sansom to the Deputy Director of the Office of Far Eastern Affairs Dr. Joseph W. Ballantine, February 26, 1944.

Intelligence Proposal, n.d., *Folder 3, Box 319, Entry 210, RG 226*, USNA.

Khana Ratsadon, Khana Ratsadon Announcement Issue 1. (คณะราษฎร, ประกาศคณะราษฎร ฉบับที่ ๑)

Library of Congress, Federal Research Division, Country Profile: Thailand, (Washington D.C.: Library of Congress, 2007).

M. Coultas (B), 16 May 1939, F5250.

M.J.R. Talbout in Foreign Office minutes, 21 June 1939, F6310.

M.R. Seni Praoj, manuscript of a speech given 17 August 1946, unpaged.

Robert W. Lawson, "General Report of the Situation in Bangkok," October 9, 1945, *Folder 274, Box 24, Entry 110, RG 226*, USNA.

Senate Resolution 9 (1960). 115th Congress 1st Session.

Suphasawat to Seni, 14 May 1942, FO 371-31862-3953, PRO.

U.S. State Department Libraries – Consulate General of the United States of America, Chiang Mai, Thailand, *Two Nations One Friendship 180 Years*, May 2013.

"2011 United Nations' International Convention on the Elimination of All Forms of Racial Discrimination". Report submitted by the Royal Thai Government to the United Nations.

About the Author

Wantakan Nicolette Arcado, known by her friends as Nickii, is the author of *Reclamation and Recentralization in Southeast Asia* in the 8th edition of the Berkeley Student Journal of Asian Studies. She graduated from the University of California, Berkeley with a Bachelor's degree in Political Science. Originally from Udon Thani, Thailand, she now lives in the Bay Area. Her goal is to work in foreign policy and continue improving international relations between her home countries of Thailand and the United States.

www.ingramcontent.com/pod-product-compliance
Lightning Source LLC
Chambersburg PA
CBHW032037040426
42449CB00007B/930